THE ONE WHO HID AWAY

THREE FRENCH SAINTS
THE ONE WHO HID AWAY

Thérèse of Lisieux
(1873-1897)

Críostóir Ó Floinn

the columba press

First published in 2009 by
the columba press
55A Spruce Avenue, Stillorgan Industrial Park,
Blackrock, Co Dublin

Cover by Bill Bolger
Origination by The Columba Press
Printed by Athenaeum Press, Gateshead

ISBN 978-1-85607-657-9

Table of Contents

CHAPTER ONE

A Saint Revealed

On 30 September 1897 a twenty-four-year old nun named Sister Thérèse of the Child Jesus died of tuberculosis in a convent of the Carmelites, an enclosed order, in the city of Lisieux in France. She had entered the convent at the exceptionally young age of fifteen. She was unknown to the world outside the convent, except for some relations – her parents were already deceased – and was considered by some of her sisters in religion as an ordinary nun whose short life in the order was not marked by anything unusual, so much so that, shortly before she died, one of them wondered what could be said of her in the brief biographical notice which it was customary to distribute to other houses of the order on the death of a nun.

In 1925, just twenty-seven years after her death, Pope Pius XI officially proclaimed this young nun a saint – she was already long canonised by *vox populi*. One hundred years after her death, Pope John Paul II bestowed on this young woman, who had lived and died unknown to the world, the title Doctor of the Church, thus declaring to the Catholic world that her spiritual teaching and way of life were to be regarded as having contributed significantly to the understanding, by clergy and laity alike, of the theology and spirituality of the Catholic faith. Not only did this make her one of only three women among the thirty-three saints thus honoured – her own patron saint and founder of the Reformed Carmelites, Teresa of Avila (1515-1582) and St Catherine of Siena (1347-1380) counsellor of popes and kings, were both given the title in 1970 – but it placed the young nun of Lisieux on the same exalted plane as theological sages like St Thomas Aquinas. Evidence of this is to be found in the official *Catechism of the Catholic Church* published in 1994 and based on the doctrinal and catechetical discussions of the Second Vatican

Council. In several sections of the *Catechism*, quotations from St Thérèse of Lisieux are used both to illustrate points of doctrine and as a source of encouragement to the faithful. Even her personal definition of prayer is given precedence over the more formally theological one of St John Damascene that had been in use since the fifth century.

While popes and theologians were thus acknowledging officially that a girl who desired only to hide herself away from the world in a life of prayer and sacrifice had been chosen by the Holy Spirit to be an instrument of grace and renewal in the church of Christ, the hidden nun of Lisieux was becoming one of the most popular saints in the devotional manifestations of the faithful everywhere. Under the familiar title of the 'Little Flower', deriving from her own description of herself as merely a little white flower of the Child Jesus, she was taken to their hearts by all kinds of people, from intellectuals like Paul Claudel, Edith Stein and Thomas Merton, to the very children making their First Holy Communion. Her statue, along with that other favourite, St Anthony of Padua, was to be found in almost every Catholic church in the world, and she was prayed to probably more than any heavenly intercessor except Our Blessed Lady herself. Miracles physical and spiritual were being attributed to her, and in many countries there were societies and magazines promoting devotion to a saint who seemed to have been specially provided by God for the technologically enriched but spiritually impoverished world of the twentieth century. In the middle of that century, in 1954, after the Second World War had shown once again the madness that afflicts the human race when it ignores its Creator, the Basilica of Sainte Thérèse was consecrated in Lisieux and became a place of popular pilgrimage in the very town where she had tried to hide away from the world and be known only to God.

How did this extraordinary metamorphosis come about? To answer that question, let us go back in imagination to the last decade of the nineteenth century and to that enclosed Carmelite convent in the town of Lisieux in France.

CHAPTER TWO

The Making of a Book

There were two items about this small Carmelite convent that were unusual. The Carmelite rule stated that no more than two members of a family should normally be accepted in the same convent. It also laid down the age of entry as twenty-one. In this convent at Lisieux, in 1895, there were twenty-five nuns of whom four were blood sisters from the Martin family, and the youngest of these, Thérèse, had been accepted as a postulant when she was only a few months over fifteen years of age. It is through these unusual factors that, on a winter's evening in 1895, the process is to begin which will make the life and holiness of Sister Thérèse of the Child Jesus known to the outside world and will culminate in her canonisation in 1925 by Pope Pius XI.

In 1895, the year to which the time-machine of our imagination has brought us back, Sister Thérèse was twenty-two years old, while the second eldest of her three sisters, Pauline – in religion Mother Agnes of Jesus – was thirty-four. She had been the first of the four to enter Carmel, and she was now Prioress, having been elected two years earlier for the statutory term of three years. In her evidence at the official process for the beatification of the girl who had been her baby sister, she recalled what happened on that fateful evening when the nuns were gathered for their recreation period in the only room of the convent that had a fireplace.

> One evening in the beginning of the year 1895, two and a half years before the death of Sister Thérèse, I was with my two sisters, Marie and Thérèse. Sister Thérèse of the Child Jesus told us several events of her childhood and

Sister Marie of the Sacred Heart (my eldest sister Marie) said to me: 'O Mother, what a pity that all this should not be written down for us! If you were to ask Sister Thérèse of the Child Jesus to write down her childhood memories, how much pleasure this would give us!' So, I then turned to Sister Thérèse of the Child Jesus, who was laughing as though we were teasing her, and I said to her: 'I order you to write down your memories of your childhood.'

Although Thérèse pointed out that there could hardly be anything in what she might write that was not already known to her sisters, she must have recounted some incidents or conversations of which they had no recollection; also, of course, they had been in boarding-school as teenagers when their baby sister was growing up. On the other hand, Thérèse quotes at length in her manuscript from letters written by their mother to the two older girls, Marie and Pauline, while they were in boarding school. In these letters 'Mamma' fondly recounts incidents about the two younger children, Thérèse and Céline; so, these letters must have been given to her by Mother Agnes (Pauline) herself as a source of further material.

The spontaneous suggestion, later an order, from Mother Agnes might also have been a result of the fact that Thérèse had already shown a flair for writing, albeit in the confined area of prayers and pious poems, as well as some religious plays for the entertainment of the community – just then she was writing a second play about her inspirational favourite historical character, Jeanne d'Arc. Neither Thérèse herself nor her sisters could have suspected, as they sat around the fire with other nuns in the community room of that small convent in Lisieux, that the Holy Spirit was just then sending a spark on earth that would develop into a worldwide flame of spirituality and devotion.

In obedience to her Mother Superior who was also her big sister, Thérèse set to work in conditions that would have appalled any famous French writer who might just then have been commencing his next novel or play. Although the great Saint Teresa of Avila wrote an autobiography and some other books, her reform of the Carmelite rule was not designed with the view of allowing leisure for literary composition. Between rising at 4.45 am and retiring at 10.30 pm the daily routine was one of prayer and work, interspersed with meals and a few periods of community recreation. For this new task imposed on her by religious obedience, Thérèse had to use some of the short moments of rest that her declining health needed so badly. She wrote on pages taken from some exercise copies, sitting on a bench with an old writing-desk on her knees, and by the light of a small and faulty paraffin lamp. On 20 January 1896, a year after being ordered to write it, she delivered the manuscript to Mother Agnes. Its simple form seemed suited to the prescribed content, a reminiscence of childhood; it consisted of six booklets sewn together, comprising about 170 pages in all.

If Thérèse expected a sisterly reaction of appreciation and delight, even if tinged with some gentle criticism, she must have been disappointed. What she got was total silence. Mother Agnes, as Prioress, seems to have been too busy to read the work she had ordered her little sister to produce. She put it aside and did not read it until two months later. By then, her period as Prioress had come to an end and, as an ordinary nun, she had less official care and more free time. She showed the work to her sisters, but did not show it to the nun who had replaced her as Prioress, Mother Marie de Gonzague – a much older nun between whom and the Martin sisters there was continuous and unedifying tension – until 2 June 1897, more than a year after receiving it from its author, who at this point had just four months more to live.

By that time, a second and very different manuscript had been added to the first. On reading the first manuscript, the older Martin sisters would have realised that it was more than just a factual narration of the childhood memories of Thérèse. In fact, even the opening sentence indicates that the request-cum-order from Mother Agnes (Pauline) must have suggested a more comprehensive and meditative approach (it should be noted that after their mother's death, when Thérèse was only four years old, she had regarded her big sister, Pauline, as her 'second mother').

The manuscript begins thus: 'Dearest Mother, it is to you, who are my mother twice over, that I am going to tell the history of my soul.' That sentence, by the way, would subsequently provide the title, *The Story of a Soul*, for the autobiography published after her death. The first two pages are a spiritual reflection, concluding with the lovely thought: 'Everything conspires for the good of each individual soul, just as the march of the seasons is designed to make the most insignificant daisy unfold its petal on the day appointed for it.' And then Thérèse comes back to earth and to the task in hand: 'Dear Mother, you must be wondering by now what all this is leading up to; not a word yet to suggest that I am telling the story of my life! But, you see, you told me to write down, without reserve, all the thoughts which came into my mind, and it isn't exactly an account of my life that I mean to write; these are the thoughts which occur to me about the graces which God in his mercy has seen fit to grant me. I am now at a moment in my life when I can afford to look back at the past. The fire of sufferings, outward and inward, has brought me to maturity; I am like a flower that can lift its head, refreshed, after the storm has passed by.'

It was no surprise, then, to the author's sisters, that the narrative of her childhood years was interlaced with the spiritual reflections and comments of the twenty-four-year old nun, Sister Thérèse of the Child Jesus, whose wisdom and holiness had so impressed the Prioress, Mother Marie de Gonzague, that she had been entrusted with the direction of the five novices. In September 1896, a few months after being shown the first manuscript, Marie (Sister Marie of the Sacred Heart), the eldest sister and godmother of Thérèse, asked her to write an account of her ideas on the religious life and the way to holiness as she had been teaching them to the novices and incidentally to the community in conversation, as well as through her poems and plays. Thérèse replied in ten closely written pages, her deteriorating health evident in the many corrections. The first three pages were addressed to Sister Marie, the remaining seven were in the form of a mystical monologue to Jesus.

The third part of what was to become *The Story of a Soul* was written in the last months of the author's life. Its origin, like the first part, is best told in the words of Mother Agnes as recorded at the process for the beatification of her sister, Thérèse, words that reveal something of the tension between the current and the previous holders of the office of Prioress:

> It seemed to me that these accounts were incomplete. Sister Thérèse of the Child Jesus had concentrated on her childhood and early youth as I had asked her to do, her life as a nun was hardly sketched in ... I thought it a great pity that she had not described the development of her life in the Carmel in the same way, but just then I ceased to be Reverend Mother and Mother Marie de Gonzague held this office. I was afraid she would not attach the same interest as I did to these writings and I dared not say anything about it. But then, seeing that Sister Thérèse was so ill, I determined to try the impossible. About midnight on the evening of the second of June 1897, four months before the death of Sister Thérèse, I went to see Mother Prioress. 'Mother,' I said, 'I can't go to sleep without having told you a secret. When I was Prioress, Sister Thérèse, in order to please me and by obedience, wrote down some recollections of her childhood. I re-read them the other day. They are charming, but you will not get much out of them to help you compose her Circular after her death, because they contain very little about her life as a religious. If you were to order her to do so, she could write something more valuable, and I don't doubt that you would have something incomparably better than I have.' God blessed my action and the next morning Reverend Mother ordered Sister Thérèse of the Child Jesus to go on with her account.

Whereas the first or 'family' manuscript had been written on odd pages, and the second on squared writing-paper, for this third section, addressed to Mother Marie de Gonzague, Sister Thérèse was provided with a copy-book of good quality, bound in black oil-cloth. As it was mid-summer, Thérèse was able to spend much of the day in the open, but her writing was hindered by her physical weakness – she had been coughing up blood since the previous year – and also, as she wryly records, by the well-intentioned interruptions of nuns, coming and going about tasks like the haymaking, who thought that a little chat would cheer her up. As she grew weaker, Thérèse could write only in pencil. Eventually, although she would live for two months more, on a day early in July 1897, the pencil fell from her hand. The last word she wrote was love. In fact, it is the final word in all three manuscripts. Readers of what is generally considered to be the greatest poetic work ever written, the *Divina Commedia* by Dante Alighieri (1265-1321), will recall that the three sections of his imaginative journey through *Inferno*, *Purgatorio* and *Paradiso* all end with the word *stelle* (stars). In the case of the great Italian poet, it was his genius and his love of poetic form that consciously arranged this significant factor; in the case of the dying young French nun, there cannot have been any deliberate effort to achieve such an effect – in fact, the final sentence is not even finished. It is as if the Holy Spirit put God's own seal on the three sections of her autobiography by ending them with the very word that encapsulates all her saintly life and spiritual teaching.

Thérèse died on 30 September 1897. Her sister Pauline, Mother Agnes, added further material to the three manuscripts already in existence by recording her words during her last days. It was now obvious to all concerned that, not only was there enough and more material to compile the Circular or biographical notice which it was customary to send to other convents on the death of a nun, but also that something unique and important existed in the pages written by the recently deceased Sister Thérèse of the Child Jesus. At first in the familial conversations of the surviving three Martin sisters – joined since August

1870, by their first cousin, Marie Guérin – and then among the other nuns, the idea began to develop that these disparate writings of Sister Thérèse might be made into a unified text that could prove of spiritual benefit to a wider readership than the nuns themselves.

It is clear from the notes made by Mother Agnes that in her final months Thérèse herself was thinking on these lines, although she dismissed with a smile the suggestion that her spiritual writings might even be sent to Rome as a matter of interest to the Holy Father himself – the suggestion itself indicates that some at least of those caring for and praying with the dying nun must have believed that they were in the presence of a saint. She entrusted to Mother Agnes the care and any necessary editing of her writings, saying: 'I have not had time to write what I have wished to write. Is isn't complete ... anything you want to take out from or add to the note-book of my life, it is as though I myself were cutting or adding.' Thérèse also said prophetically, 'Everyone will see that it all comes from the good God, and whatever fame I may have will be a gratuitous gift which will not belong to me; this will be quite clear to all.'

When the family sisters of Thérèse decided that, instead of the customary biographical document, her own autobiographical manuscripts should be combined into an actual book for distribution to the other Carmelite convents, Mother Agnes had first of all to obtain permission for this from the Prioress, Mother Gonzague, with whom, as has been noted, she was not on the best of terms. Mother Gonzague, herself an ardent believer in the sanctity of Sister Thérèse, gave permission – but with the strange proviso that all three manuscripts were to be altered so that they would be addressed personally to herself. Apart from the tedious fulfilment of this injunction, Mother Agnes also undertook the more complicated task of editing the various writings of Thérèse so as to form what would become the book now known as *Histoire d'une âme (The Story of a Soul)*.

When Mother Agnes went to work on the various writings, she amended the punctuation and syntax, as well as minor linguistic lapses, but she also took literally Thérèse's permission to cut and add where she thought it necessary. Besides making excisions when she thought some material repetitive or of little interest, she rewrote or added to passages in order to clarify their content. She also, obviously with the permission of Mother Gonzague, added some of Thérèse's letters and poems to the three manuscripts. Before the book could be printed, however, a further permission had to be obtained – the bishop had to give the necessary *Imprimatur*. Mother Gonzague decided to use an intermediary in the person of the Prior of the Abbey of Mondaye, Rev Godefroy Madelaine, a friend of the community who had known Sister Thérèse and who was himself the author of a biography of Saint Norbert. Having read the text, he marked some suggested cuts and alterations, especially the omission of some of the family details and anecdotes in the first manuscript, which he felt would not be of general interest, and also of some of the passages of mystical spirituality which he deemed 'daring … and too far above the ordinary level'. Thirty years later, in a letter to Mother Agnes herself, he recalled that his opinions on the latter caused her to *sauter au plafond* ('hit the ceiling') and were firmly rejected by her.

When Dom Madelaine presented the manuscript to the bishop for his approval, that dignitary's first reaction was to tell him that one should always be careful in dealing with the imagination of women. Although the bishop eventually gave the official permission to print the book, he refused to supply an introduction. It was Dom Madelaine himself who wrote the introduction; he also divided the text into chapters and suggested replacing the titles proposed by Mother Agnes, one formal, the other poetic, with *Histoire d'une âme écrite par elle-même (The story of a soul written by herself)*, the first three words eventually becoming the accepted form.

When Dom Madelaine returned the mss to Mother Agnes, the nuns had to write out a clean and clear copy of the by now much-marked pages of various kinds before the book could be sent to the printer. When the book became known to a world-

wide readership, and especially when the cause of the beatification of Thérèse was going forward, it also became known that
the text as printed was not exactly what she had written; inevitably, then, the demand grew for a new edition that would
give the very words of Thérèse herself. The original texts had already been supplied to Rome for official scrutiny, but the person
who prevented publication to the world at large, even after
Thérèse had been canonised, was Mother Agnes herself, she
who had lovingly laboured to prepare the original version of *The
Story of a Soul*. She had been appointed Prioress for life and she
worried about the disputes and controversies that might ensue
about the texts. In 1947, the Bishop of Bayeux and Lisieux gave
permission for the publication of the original texts, and the
Definitor General of the Carmelites himself wrote to Mother
Agnes urging her to co-operate. However, in deference to her
age and position, a decree from Rome supported her decision
that the original texts would not be published until after her
death. She then appointed her sister, Céline (Sister Geneviève),
to take charge of what would be the verbatim facsimile edition
of the works of their sister, Saint Thérèse.

Mother Agnes died in July 1951, and a year later the decree of
the Holy See was lifted. The way was then clear for the production of the long-awaited publication of the original texts of St
Thérèse. Much of the preliminary work had already been done
by Sister Geneviéve and her helpers in the Lisieux Carmel, but
the nuns entrusted the formal and final edition of the work to a
renowned Carmelite scholar, Fr Gabriel de Sainte-Marie-
Madeleine, who had for long been involved in the proposed
new edition. Unfortunately, he died within a year of the
Vatican's lifting of its decree. His replacement was an erudite
and literary Carmelite colleague, Fr Françoise de Sainte-Marie,
who finally produced, in 1956, the facsimile edition to replace
the version edited by Mother Agnes in 1898. Like its predeces-
sor, this new edition of *Histoire d'une âme* was translated into
many languages – the English version was done by Monsignor
Robert Knox, like Newman an Oxford scholar and convert – and

maintained the prestige and popularity of the original edition. In his introduction to the new edition, Fr Françoise stated that he had found over seven thousand variations 'from the smallest to the most important' in the 1989 edition from what Thérèse had actually written, but as later scholars have pointed out, this included even the formal correction of punctuation and spelling. A more serious charge brought against Fr Françoise is that he decided to alter the sequence of the three manuscripts of Thérèse, inserting the spirtually mystical letter to her sister, Marie-Louise (Sister Marie of the Sacred Heart) between the two autobiographical texts, the first originally addressed to Pauline (Mother Agnes), the second to Mother Gonzague. In a recent critical edition of the texts, which restores the original sequence, the Belgian Carmelite scholar, P. Conrad de Meester, discusses these matters in learned detail (*Histoire d'une âme, Nouvelle edition critique,* Presses de la Renaissance, Paris, 2005).

For the general reader, however, the well-intentioned alterations made to the text in preparing the original edition of 1898 did not affect the spiritual and doctrinal teaching of Saint Thérèse. Readers of *The Story of a Soul* during the fifty years after its first publication, while unaware that they were not reading word for word what Thérese had actually written on paper, were not prevented in any way from gaining from the book the spiritual benefit and encouragement envisaged by Thérèse herself and by all concerned in making her various writings available to the world outside the walls of the Carmelite convent in Lisieux.

The cost of printing the book was borne by Isidore Guérin, uncle of the Martin sisters and father of Marie Guérin who had entered the convent of Lisieux in 1895 and had been a novice under Sister Thérèse (as will be seen later, he had initally opposed, on grounds of age, the entry of Thérèse herself). The nuns ordered two thousand copies of the book from a local printer, but being aware that many such books about pious lives ended up as waste paper, they worried that the amount might be too optimistic. The book was published on 30 September 1898.

CHAPTER TWO

Mother Agnes recalled later that some Carmelite convents commented unfavourably. When the book was read aloud in the refectory of the convent in which its author had lived and died, there were some sisters eating in silence there who must have winced on recognising the little mishaps and personal foibles which Thérèse, without naming names, had recorded as being occasions for her practice of patience and charity. Otherwise, however, *The Story of a Soul* became the story of a bestseller. The first printing had to be repeated quickly. Nearly 50,000 copies were sold in the ten years after publication. It had already sold millions by the time when the death of Mother Agnes in 1951 made the way clear for the production of the original text, a task she herself, as has been seen, formally entrusted by her to her sister, Céline, Sister Geneviéve of the Sacred Heart, then the only surviving member of the Martin family. Today, *Histoire d'une âme* has been translated into more than sixty languages and has gone through nearly a hundred editions, while the number of books written about the life and spiritual teaching of Saint Thérèse of Lisieux runs into many thousands

CHAPTER THREE

A Nursery of Sainthood

An amusing and thought-provoking film entitled, *Trading Places*, was based on the socio-psychological question whether heredity or environment is the greater influence on the individual human being. The childhood of St Thérèse provides evidence in favour of the combined effect of the two factors, God's grace, of course, being a third and mysterious factor. If ever a person was destined to become a saint, purely as a result of being the child of saintly parents and being reared in a pious environment, that person was the child born to Louis and Zélie (née Guérin) Martin in Alençon, France, on 2 January 1873. She was their ninth and last child – three had already died in infancy and one at five years old. She was christened Marie Françoise Thérèse.

Above the graves of St Thérèse's parents behind the Basilica in Lisieux one reads words written by her a few months before she died: 'God gave me a father and mother more worthy of heaven than of earth.' The fact that Louis and Zélie Martin have themselves been beatified as I write this book is sufficient proof that the verdict of their youngest child is corroborated by the diocesan investigation into the sanctity of their lives as individuals and as parents.

The first thing to be said about them as the parents of a saint is that neither of them chose marriage as their first option; they had both felt the call to the religious life and had both been rejected. When their five surviving daughters all became nuns – although the mother was in heaven even before the first one entered Carmel – it was proof of the ancient religious maxim, 'God's ways are not our ways' and of its modern folk version, 'Man proposes, but God disposes.'

The families of Louis and Zélie were of the Normandy region

of France, and both their fathers were soldiers, although Zélie's father had retired from the army and become a gendarme before she was born in the town of Alençon two days before Christmas in 1831. Louis was not born in Normandy but in Bordeaux in the south-west of France where his father, Captain Martin, was stationed at the time. Of his siblings, an older brother died at sea as a young man, a sister died in her twenties, while a younger sister died aged nine. Another sister, Annie, lived to marry and have a son, but died when, like her own young sister, her son was only nine years old. Louis Martin thus had already experienced the ravages of early death among his siblings before he and Zélie had to bury four of their own children.

Captain Martin was transferred from Bordeaux to Avignon, and later to Strasbourg, his last posting, where he spent two years, 1828-1830, and where Louis made the acquaintance of the German language. On retirement, Captain Martin returned to his native Normandy and settled with his family in Alençon. In 1842, at the age of nineteen, his son, Louis, went to Rennes in Brittany to learn the trade of watchmaking from his father's cousin. He already had a good knowledge of French literature, and he now acquired a love for Breton culture and music. A year later he went to Strasbourg, where he had lived for two years as a boy, to continue his apprenticeship. On the way, he paid a visit to the Augustinian monastery of Mount St Bernard in the Swiss Alps. Somewhere he picked a little white flower which he kept all his life and which was to have a significance he could not foresee. After two years in Strasbourg, he set out for home. Once more he visited the Monastery of Mount St Bernard, not now as a tourist but as an applicant for admission to the monastic life. The Prior regretfully told him that he could not be accepted because of an insufficient knowledge of Latin, but encouraged him to return when that essential requirement was added to his qualifications.

On his return to Alençon, Louis set to work at once to remedy this deficiency, but a bout of illness intervened and on recovery he realised he had lost his appetite for the study of the official language of the church. He decided then that God wished him to live a life of piety as a layman, and he resumed his study of watchmaking at a higher level in Paris. In November 1850, now a master in the craft, he returned to Alençon and set up a shop, bringing his parents to live with him in the large house. Later he added a jeweller's shop. His reputation as an honest and reliable businessman spread and brought prosperity to the extent that he was able to buy himself a small property outside the town, called the Pavilion, as a quiet place of rest, reading and prayer. In the garden there he installed a statue of Our Lady which, like the little white flower from the Alps, was to be of further significance in his life. In his free time he was active in works of charity, and he also enjoyed his hobbies of reading and fishing – from the latter pastime, the nuns in the local convent of the Poor Clares were often the beneficiaries. And so, Louis Martin settled down to a pleasant and comfortable life as a devout and charitable intellectual bachelor. He did not know that his mother, and the Holy Spirit, had other plans for him.

Louis' mother had long been praying that he would meet and marry what all such loving mothers call 'the right girl'. Now, eight years after she and her husband had moved in to live with him, Mme Martin was attending a lace-making class in the town. There she put her maternal eye on an attractive and pleasant young woman named Zélie Guérin, whose father, like her own husband, was a retired military man. Having got to know her sufficiently, she became convinced that this was the God-sent ideal wife for her son. She contrived an encounter which resulted in the result she had prayed for. Three months later, on 13 July 1858, Zélie and Louis were married – it was the year of the apparitions at Lourdes, the last of the series occurring three days after that wedding in Alençon. Louis was 35, Zélie 27, when they settled in to domestic life in spacious rooms behind the shop, while his parents occupied a separate apartment on the floor above.

Like her new husband, Zélie Guérin had felt a call to the religious life, but she had been refused by the Sisters of Charity of St

Vincent de Paul because of her poor health – as a child, she had suffered respiratory problems and severe headaches. Her disappointment was compounded by the fact that her only sister, Marie Louise, two years her senior, entered the Visitation Convent at Le Mans at the age of 29, only two months before Zélie's marriage. Their only brother, Isidore, who was ten years younger than Zélie, after having studied medicine in Paris, opened a pharmacy in Lisieux where he and his wife were destined to prove supportive neighbours to his widowed brother-in-law, Louis Martin, and his five daughters.

Zélie spoke of her childhood as having been unhappy and 'as sad as a winding-sheet'. Her mother was a devout woman but not affectionate; she was so strict that she would not allow the girls to have dolls. The father, having been both a soldier and a policeman, was also strict but kinder. After they moved to Alençon, when Zélie was thirteen, her mother ran a café in the town for some years. Her father, however, sold his land and house outside the town in order to ensure that the children got a good education, the two girls with the nuns, the only son, Isidore, at the local Lycée and later at Paris to study medicine. Zélie was noted by her teachers as intelligent and pious, and she took first place in her French studies. She was also skilful and artistic, two qualities which led to her rapid progress when she began those lessons in lace-making; so rapid, in fact, that she soon went into business herself. When she married Louis Martin in 1858, she set up her office beside his shop. Her lace enterprise matched her husband's success in watchmaking and jewellery; soon she was employing other women in their own homes, sometimes as many as twenty, to make pieces which she would then combine into designs of her own creation. While being a loving and devoted wife and mother, she was also a shrewd and energetic businesswoman who studied the stock market and investments.

Above all else, however, Zélie Guérin, the young woman whose heartfelt desire it had been to devote her life to God in a religious order, was the soul-companion in faith, religious observance, and charity, of the devout Louis Martin, a man who had harboured the same longing in his youth. Marriage for such a couple was a change of life more complicated than it usually is for less spiritually-orientated souls. At first, they agreed to live in chastity, an arrangement aided by Zélie's fear of the problems of childbirth. In the meantime, their charity led them to care for a poor boy of five, one of a large family whose father had died. However, after ten months of this unusual form of married bliss, their confessor counselled them that God would rather see them creating children of their own according to the divine plan for the human race. This counsel they accepted, presumably with natural joy as a bonus on their religious assent. The fulfilment of motherhood caused Zélie to write later, 'I simply love children. I think I was born for this.' In the next thirteen years nine children were born, seven girls and two boys. Sadly, as has been seen, although honoured in being chosen by God to be the mothers of saints – an honour they would not enjoy until they were in heaven – both Zélie Martin in Alençon and Louise Soubirous in Lourdes also had in common the recurring sorrow of seeing several others of their children die in infancy or at a very young age. They themselves also died young, Louise Soubirous at 41, Zélie Martin at 46.

The first child of Zélie and Louis Martin was a girl, born on 22 February 1860. They named her Marie Louise – they had decided that any children God gave them would have Our Lady's name along with that of their individual patron. The second child, Marie Pauline, was born on 7 September 1861. The third child, Marie Léonie, was born on 3 June 1863. She suffered from measles and convulsions as a baby, but survived and was later to prove the most problematic of the children. The fourth child, Marie Hélène, was born on 13 October 1864, and had to be given over to a wet nurse as Zélie's health was already giving cause for concern. Although a healthy child, she fell ill suddenly and died at the age of five.

The fifth child, the first son, was born on 20 September 1866 and named Marie Joseph Louis. He was strong and healthy, and

Zélie prayed he might fulfil her great desire to have a son a priest. This child also had to be entrusted to the wet nurse, Rose Taillé, who lived on a farm seven miles from Alençon. Like the previous child, however, he contracted a sudden illness and died on 14 February 1867, only five months old. The sixth child, a second son, Marie Joseph Jean Baptiste, was born a week before Christmas in that same year, 1867. It was the most difficult birth of all, and the baby was so ill that the doctor baptised him. Although nursed for a few months by Rose Taillé, he never gained strength and died on 24 August 1868, in his mother's arms. Two weeks later, Zélie's father died – she had brought him to live with them on the death of her mother. At this time also her sister, Marie, was dying of tuberculosis in the convent of the Visitation at Le Mans, where the two eldest Martin girls were now boarders.

The seventh child was another daughter, Marie Céline, born on 28 April 1869. She had to be given to a different wet nurse, and Zélie feared that she might not survive; but it was the five-year-old Hélène who suddenly fell ill and died at this time. Céline was four years older than Thérèse, but was the last of the four Martin sisters who would enter Carmel. She entered in 1894, at the age of twenty-five, having cared for her ailing father until his death.

The eighth child, Marie Melanie Thérèse, was born on 16 August 1870. Finding a wet nurse for her proved a problem, and when she died at the age of two months it was considered that the wet nurse to whom she had been eventually entrusted had virtually starved the baby to death.

With the birth of her ninth child, another girl, Zélie must have realised with sadness and resignation that, because of the serious deterioration in her health, this would be her final child, and so her hope of having a son a priest would not now be fulfilled. She did not know that God was giving her and her husband, Louis, the care of a future saint. This baby of destiny was born on 2 January 1873, and christened Marie-Françoise Thérèse two days later in Notre Dame church in Alençon, with her eldest sister, Marie, as her godmother.

Twenty-two years later, in 1895, when she began, in compliance with the order from her sister, Pauline, to write the story of her life, Sister Thérèse of the Child Jesus summed up the devout and loving family milieu into which she was born. In a poetic passage that uses the lily, traditional symbol of purity, to signify that milieu, she wrote:

> I am very glad to be able to put on record the favours Our Lord has shown me, all quite undeserved … It was he that chose the soil I was to grow up in, holy ground, all steeped, as one might say, in the scent of purity. He saw to it that eight lilies of dazzling whiteness should grow up there before me … And what of our parents, the blessed stock from which we all sprang? They have been reunited, for all eternity, in their heavenly country, and found there, waiting for them, those four lilies that never unfolded fully to earthly eyes. May Jesus be merciful to us, who are still in exile here, and not leave us long on this alien shore.

CHAPTER FOUR

The Happy Years

It was Thérèse herself who described the years from 'the dawn of reason in me to the day when our dear Mother left us for a better home in heaven', when Thérèse was still not five years old, as the happiest period of her life before she entered Carmel at the age of fifteen. Readers of *The Story of a Soul* will find, however, that her description of that part of her life is hampered by two factors.

The first was acknowledged by herself at the outset when she protested to her sisters in Carmel: 'What can I write that you do not already know?' Her point seems proven by the many incidents she relates about her early years which are quoted from their mother's letters to Pauline at boarding-school, letters which, as we have seen, must have been lovingly kept by Pauline and later supplied to Thérèse as an aid to her reminiscence. Many of the incidents she relates are about herself and Céline, four years older and her constant companion. Many are also, inevitably, similar to stories that could be told by the mother of any large family, ranging from childish questions or surmisings to amusing or worrying mishaps and misdemeanours. In a devout Catholic family like the Martins, there are also, as would be expected, stories about the pious practices of Thérèse and her naïve thoughts about God and heaven.

The second consideration that must have constricted the flow of Thérèse's thought and pen was that she was a nun writing for her colleagues in an enclosed convent. Although she says at the outset, addressing her sister and Prioress, 'It's for you only that I mean to write down the story of the little flower Jesus has picked; so, I can talk to you quite freely', she must have known, even at that point, that eyes other than those of her family sisters were likely to read those pages. Even for the eyes of her sisters, her good sense, apart from the general rule of charity, must have guided her into the omission of any less happy incidents of family life, such as can result from stress, illness, conflict of personality or opinion. She is clearly conscious of the obligation, in this family manuscript, to say only nice things about everyone, and Mother Agnes (Pauline), is thought to have suggested the insertion of a line here or there in that regard, even about their Uncle Isidore Guérin and his wife, Céline, to whom she later sent a copy of the manuscript for their comments.

Thérèse makes a point of remembering especially her sister, Léonie, who was ten years older and had been considered, even in their mother's letters, to be a cause of worry (she had also chosen to enter a different order). 'And, of course, little Léonie,' Thérèse says, 'of whom I was also very fond. And she was so fond of me – when the rest of the family went out for a walk in the evening, it was she who looked after me. I can still hear the soft lullabies with which she used to put me to sleep. She was determined to keep me happy at all costs, and for my part, I should have hated to cause her the least uneasiness.'

It is worth noting that when Léonie, at the age of 31 and at the second attempt, entered the Visitation Order at Caen in 1894, just three years before the death of Thérèse, she chose the birthnames of her little sister as her name in religion and became Sister Françoise Thérèse. When *The Story of a Soul* reached her – probably from her sisters in Carmel – she adopted the spiritual teachings of Thérèse and was regarded as herself a saint by her colleagues when she died in 1941.

Two years before Thérèse was born, Louis Martin had sold his business to his nephew, Adolphe Lériche, and had begun to take an active part in the affairs of his wife's lace enterprise. The family moved to Zélie's old home where there was a large garden – Zélie conducted her business from home. A passage quoted from one of her letters to her daughter, Pauline, written in 1876 when Thérèse was three and Céline seven, illustrates the benefit of that change for the children. Zélie writes: 'Every day, immediately after dinner, Céline gets hold of her little bantam-cock, and then goes off to catch Thérèse's hen – a thing I can never do, but she's so smart she can catch it with one spring.' In the text of Thérèse's quotation of this incident, however, there is a bracketed insertion which editors assume is an explanatory note by Thérèse herself: ['It was little Rose who gave me both birds as a present, and I had given the cock to Céline']. As there is no other reference in *The Story of a Soul* to any Rose, little or big, the reader is left wondering who was this person who kindly gave such a strange present to the little Thérèse Martin living in the town of Alençon. From other sources, we learn who she was and why it was not necessary, in the case of her family sisters, for Sister Thérèse to say more, or desirable to do so if the other nuns should ever happen to read her manuscript.

The day after Thérèse was born, Zélie wrote to her sister-in-law, Céline Guérin, and said, 'She is very strong and very well … I am very happy.' She was determined, in spite of ill-health and her previous failures, to try to nurse this baby herself – the last baby girl had died due to the negligence of her wet nurse, and Zélie had decided that any future child would never run that risk; but within a few weeks things were not going well. Thérèse began to develop symptoms of serious illness such as had afflicted the babies who had not survived. After two months, the doctor warned Zélie that the baby would die if she did not find a wet nurse quickly. Louis was away on one of his now frequent business trips connected with the sales of lace; so, Zélie decided to request the services of a wet nurse whom they trusted, although she had not been able to save the lives of the two baby boys. This was a woman named Rosalie Taillé – she was already known affectionately in the Martin family as 'little Rose' – who lived with her husband and four children, the youngest a boy aged one, on a small farm at Semallé, about seven miles from Alençon. Zélie set out from the town and walked all the way to the farm where she begged Rose to come and try to save the life of her new baby girl. Having discussed the matter with her husband, Rose agreed; however, in view of her own circumstances, she had to lay down conditions: she would come and nurse Thérèse in the Martin home for an initial week, then, all being well, the baby would be brought to live with Rose's own family on the farm – and remain there for at least a year.

Zélie had no option but to agree. Rose went back with her to the Martin home in the town. At first sight, she thought the child was dead. While Rose began the first attempt to breast-feed the weakling infant, Zélie went upstairs to pray tearfully before the family statue of St Joseph, one of her favourite intercessors in heaven. When she came down after half an hour, the baby was nursing peacefully. Little Thérèse slept in Rose's arms through the night. A week later, Rose walked home to the farm, carrying her new charge well wrapped against the cold. Thérèse was to spend the first year of her life with the Taillé family, developing into a happy, healthy child; but it was an experience that would have negative as well as beneficial results.

Although Zélie visited the Taillé farm as often as her business and family cares allowed her, and Rose brought the baby to the Martin home once a week for a few hours when she, like other countrywomen, was selling produce at the market and buying supplies for her own family, inevitably Thérèse bonded more with the woman who was nursing her and with the children of the Taillé family than with her own mother and sisters. Zélie was happy to see her baby growing stronger by the week. After a few months, she wrote in a letter to her sister-in-law, 'I am very satisfied with this woman,' she wrote, 'you can hardly find another as good as her for taking care of children … Thérèse is a big baby; she is tanned by the sun. The wet-nurse brings her on a wheelbarrow into the fields, on top of loads of grass. Little Rose says you could hardly see a more lovable child.' She also noticed, however, that Thérèse was obviously more content in the arms of Rose and other countrywomen than in her own or those of any of the Martin family and their wealthy friends.

The year in the countryside, in addition to its benefit on the health of Thérèse, must also have developed in her infant sensitivity that love of nature in all its aspects that would be strengthened later by her father when he took her on walks in the country or as his little companion when he went fishing – she describes how she used to sit dreamily observing the flowers and the sky while he tried his luck with rod and line. When Thérèse, now fifteen months old, was brought back to the family home in Alençon, however, she became disturbed and troublesome at finding herself suddenly separated from the family and surroundings that had become part of her daily existence. It took a long time, and a lot of patience and loving understanding on the part of her real parents and family, before she adjusted, with growing awareness as she increased in age, to her new life in the town.

Sister Thérèse of the Child Jesus must have been unpleasantly surprised when she read some of her mother's letters to big sister Pauline in the boarding school; she humbly copied some of them into the manuscript she was now writing for the same sister. Writing of her at the toddler stage, Zélie had this to say:

At the moment, Céline is playing bricks to amuse Baby. Every now and then they start arguing, but Céline gives way; another pearl (she thinks) for her crown. Baby, when things aren't going well for her, gets pitiably worked up, so that I have to talk her round; she seems to think that all is lost, and sometimes the feeling is too much for her, and she chokes with indignation. She's such a very excitable child, and yet she's quite good and very intelligent; she remembers everything she's told.

In another letter, a few months after Thérèse's homecoming, her mother described her as 'a little burden at times' and given to 'frightful tantrums'. She went on, incidentally revealing something of her own lifestyle: 'She is continually at my feet, and it is difficult for me to work. So, to make up for the time lost, I continue my lace-work until ten at night, and I rise at five o'clock. I still have to get up once or twice during the night for the little one. However, the more trouble I have, the better I am.'

Even when she was more than two years old, Thérèse still felt so insecure that when going up the stairs she used to stop on each step and call out, 'Mamma! Mamma!', refusing to move again until she heard her mother's loving voice in reply.

As an illustration of what she considers her faults of self-esteem and strong will even at an early age, Thérèse relates an incident 'which Mamma doesn't mention in her letters'. Zélie was apparently trying out the strength of character she noticed developing in her youngest child when one day she playfully offered Thérèse a sou if she would kiss the ground. 'A sou was a fortune in those days,' Thérèse writes, 'and it wasn't a great loss of dignity because I wasn't much height from the ground; but no, my pride was up in arms at the idea of kissing the ground. I held myself up very straight and said: "I think not, dear Mother; I'd rather go without the sou".' Zélie confirms that strength of will in a letter in which she says, 'Once Baby has made up her mind, there's no changing her.' This is balanced, however, by another maternal comment: 'She wouldn't tell a lie for all the money in the world, and there's more originality about her than I've ever seen in any of you.'

From this troubled transitional period in her life as a child Thérèse recalls two items which, with hindsight, she regards as being of significance for her present state as a religious striving to become a saint. The first involves that middle one of the five Martin sisters, Léonie, and shows her in a more favourable light than some of the worried comments in her mother's letters. Shortly before the mother's death, the eldest sister, Marie, discovered that the behaviour of the thirteen-year-old Léonie was largely a result of physical and psychological ill-treatment by the maid, Louise. She promised her dying mother to look after Léonie, and took the first step thereto by getting her father to dismiss the maid after Zélie's death.

Thérèse describes a scene when Léonie, in her early teens and having decided she is too mature to play with dolls, offers her two younger sisters, Céline and Thérèse, a basket full of dolls' dresses and material for making more, with her own doll on top, and says, 'Here you are, darlings, choose whatever you like; they're all for you.' Céline considered and then carefully picked out a ball of silken stuff. Little Thérèse considered, and then 'I choose the whole lot!' she cried, taking over the basket. The gentle Céline, as usual, did not mind. Sister Thérèse of the Child Jesus comments on that impulsive action, 'Only a childish trait, perhaps, but in a sense it has been the key to my whole life. Later on, when the idea of religious perfection came within my horizon, I realised at once that there was no reaching sanctity unless you were prepared to suffer a great deal, to be always on the lookout for something higher still, and to forget yourself ... And then, as in babyhood, I found myself crying out: "My God, I choose the whole lot! No point in being a saint by halves ... I want everything whatsoever that is your will for me".'

She recalls also a dream she had when she was four years old. Walking in the garden, she was confronted by two terrifying little demons who, when they found that she was not afraid of them, darted here and there trying to hide from her. She comments: 'There was nothing extraordinary about this dream, but I suppose God allowed me to remember it for a special purpose. He wanted me to see that the soul, when in a state of grace, has nothing to fear from the spirits of evil; they are cowards, so cowardly that they run away at a glance from a child.'

It would seem from the generous present of the bantam cock and hen mentioned earlier that Rose Taillé kept in regular touch with the family after returning the now healthy fifteen-month-old Thérèse to her real mother; perhaps both Zélie and Rose hoped that this strange present might help the child through the transition, but the subconscious effect of loss and separation experienced in babyhood by Thérèse was to remain with her for life. A more tragic repetition of separation disrupted her young life a few years later when her mother died. When she was nine years old, a third such loss occurred when her sister, Pauline, whom she had come to regard as a replacement for her mother, became the first of the family to enter Carmel.

When she did settle into the new life in the family home at

Alençon, Thérèse found herself in an atmosphere of loving care and devout religious observance. Her parents went daily to the 5.30 am Mass, taking the older children with them when they were not in boarding school. Prayer and pious practices, including care of the poor, were part of daily life, and Louis read from a devotional book each evening. The older sisters, Marie and Pauline, started the education of the younger ones. Parents and sisters ensured that Thérèse, although the pet of the family, was not spoilt. In her manuscript reminiscence of those years, Thérèse exclaims to Pauline, 'What a happy childhood it was, Mother! I'd already begun to taste the joys of life, and at the same time virtue was, for me, something attractive.' But only a few lines later, she says: 'These sunny days of childhood, how quickly they pass!'

The happy days of childhood ended for Thérèse on 28 August 1877, the day her mother died. Ten years earlier, Zélie had consulted her pharmacist brother, Isidore, who had studied medicine in Paris, asking his advice about a painful swelling in her breast which she attributed to an injury when she was a girl. She mentioned the possibility of an operation, but for unknown reasons nothing was done at that time. In October 1876, when Thérèse was nearly four years old, the trouble flared up again and this time Zélie was told that she had a fibrous tumour for which the chances of a cure were practically nil. Among other pilgrimages, her husband Louis had once visited Lourdes and he now suggested that Zélie go there to pray for a cure – the girl whose visions of Our Lady made Lourdes a place of pilgrimage and healing, Bernadette Soubirous, was still alive, known now as Sister Marie Bernarde in the convent at Nevers; she died three years later, in 1879, when Thérèse was six years old. Unlike Louis, Zélie had no love of travelling, but she agreed to the suggestion. At this time, however, her sister, Marie Louise, a nun in the Visitation convent at Le Mans where the older Martin girls were boarders, was dying of tuberculosis; so, Zélie postponed her visit to Lourdes until after her sister's death in February of the following year.

In June 1877, she set out for Lourdes accompanied by the three eldest children, Marie, Pauline and Léonie. Apart from whatever spiritual benefit Zélie received at the grotto of the apparitions, the pilgrimage was an unhappy experience for all, beset by various mishaps and ending in understandable disappointment for the family when the mother came home obviously nearer to death than to a cure. Her condition deteriorated steadily until she died on 28 August. Her husband, Louis, who had gone to the church the day before to escort the priest bringing the Blessed Sacrament to his dying wife, prayed with the three eldest girls, and Zélie's brother Isidore and his wife, at the bedside of the saintly woman as her soul passed from this vale of tears to the presence of the God she had loved and faithfully served all through her life.

Thérèse and Céline, the two youngest, had knelt with the others when their mother received the Last Anointing and the Viaticum on the day before she died – 'All five of us were there, in order of age, and poor dear Father knelt there too, sobbing' – but they were not present at her death. Their father brought them to see Zélie in her coffin. Through the eyes of the child she was then, Thérèse describes that last scene: 'Father took me in his arms on the day of Mamma's death, or perhaps it was the day after, and said: "Come and give your poor Mother a kiss." I put my lips to dear Mother's forehead without saying a word; I don't think I was crying much; my feelings were too deep to be shared with anybody. In silence I looked and listened; nobody was bothering with me, so I was conscious of many sights that would otherwise have been spared me. Once I found myself in full view of the coffin, and stood a long time looking at it; I had never seen one before, but I understood what it all meant. Mamma was so small, and yet I had to lift my head up well before I could see the whole length of it; I hated the size of it.'

After the funeral, the five girls found themselves together in a room of the house with only the maid, Louise. She looked at the two youngest, Céline and Thérèse, and said, 'Ah, you poor little things, now you have no mother.' Upon which Céline ran to the eldest girl, Marie, and threw herself into her arms crying, 'Marie, you have to be my Mamma.' Thérèse, who always imitated Céline, then ran to Pauline, the second eldest, and declared, 'My Mamma will be Pauline.'

'I was to enter now,' Thérèse writes, 'on the second period of my life, which was also the saddest.'

CHAPTER FIVE

From Alençon to Lisieux

When his beloved Zélie died, Louis Martin, at fifty-five years of age, found himself with five daughters to provide for. Zélie's brother, Isidore Guérin, with his wife, Céline, was now living at Lisieux. On their advice, and having discussed the matter with his two eldest daughters, Marie and Pauline, Louis decided to sell the house and lace business in Alençon and move to Lisieux where the two Guérin daughters would help his own younger ones to settle in. While retaining the Pavilion near Alençon for future return visits, he leased a house called *Les Buissonets* near the Guérin home and the move was made without any apparent regrets. Thérèse records: 'I can't remember that I minded leaving Alençon; children enjoy a change, and I welcomed our arrival at Lisieux.' Louis was a comparatively wealthy man, and the new home of the Martin family was both spacious and comfortable. It is described as having three floors, with four bedrooms and three attics, and a belvedere on the third floor that had a fine view of the city; there were gardens front and rear, with a large vegetable garden, a laundry, sheds and a greenhouse. Louis made the belvedere a study for himself, where he would also receive formal visits from the two youngest girls, Céline and Thérèse, when they came to show him the marks awarded them by Marie and Pauline in their studies.

The same orderly and pious family life that had obtained at Alençon was established at Lisieux, the loss of wife and mother being counterbalanced, even if only partially, by the proximity of her brother and his family. Allowing for the fact that Sister Thérèse herself disclaims all pretensions to form and style in the composition of her manuscript reminiscences – even the great

Dante, who maintains that everything in the universe has form as a sign of its divine Creator, would make allowances for the young nun of Lisieux hampered by ill-health and circumstances – the thoughtful reader of *The Story of a Soul* will be puzzled by the anomaly that, having just stated that the period of her life after the death of her mother, from the age of four to fourteen, was the saddest of her life, Thérèse then launches into an account of what appears to be a period of four idyllic years of family life in that spacious new home in Lisieux.

The eldest girl, Marie, now aged seventeen, took charge of the housekeeping, assisted by a maid and also, no doubt, by the next in line, Pauline. Together, as they had already done at Alençon during their holidays from boarding-school, Marie and Pauline took charge of the education of the two younger girls while Léonie, the middle daughter, became a day pupil at the Benedictine school in the town. Thérèse recalls that it was Marie who taught her to write, while Pauline 'did all the rest'. The first word she learned to read, she says, was heaven, and while she enjoyed Bible history and catechism, 'there were plenty of tears over grammar – do you remember,' she asks Mother Agnes, 'the trouble about masculine and feminine?'

Louis Martin, while truly inconsolable for the loss of his beloved Zélie, was now able to live the life of a gentleman of leisure. This did not lessen his conscientious fulfilment of his duties as a loving father. He spent each evening with his daughters, chatted and played draughts with them, and had one or other of them read aloud from some well-chosen book, the evening always ending with family prayers. The two youngest he sometimes took on his knees to sing to them and tell them stories – it was to the airs she had heard from her father that Sister Thérèse later set her poems. By contrast, she relates that when they visited or stayed at the Guérin home, her well-intentioned Uncle Isidore terrified her with his deep voice and his songs about Bluebeard. It was when her father collected her from such visits that Thérèse, gazing at the starry sky, used to point at the T shape in Orion and tell him that her name was written in heaven, the prophetic import of which exclamation has not been lost on her biographers.

Louis also resumed his hobbies of fishing and travel, as a contrast to the pursuit of reading and meditation in his study. He had given up fishing during the final year of Zélie's life, and from the time he joined her in the lace business his trips away from home, to Paris and other centres, had been largely in connection with the business. As he had begun to do at Alençon, he now again took little Thérèse with him on some of his fishing trips, even supplying her with a little rod of her own; she, however, preferred as usual to study the sky and the flowers. Like the Poor Clares at Alençon, the nuns in the local Carmelite convent in Lisieux were the glad recipients of Louis' catch, if any – he could not have foreseen that the time would come when his gift to that same Carmel would be something more than a few fresh fish. Thérèse tells of a day when a sudden storm broke and, while she was enjoying the spectacle, her worried father gathered up his gear and carried his daughter on his back as he hurried home.

On afternoon walks, Louis took Thérèse to visit the Blessed Sacrament, visiting each church in the town in turn. That was how she had her first experience of Carmel. One day, when she was six years old, they visited the chapel at the Carmelite convent; her father pointed out the grille behind which, he told her, there were nuns who lived an enclosed religious life of prayer and sacrifice devoted to God – 'The suspicion never crossed my mind,' she says, 'that nine years later I should be one of them.' On those walks also, any poor person they met was given alms, Thérèse acting as the little donor. Once when they saw a man dragging himself along painfully on crutches, Thérèse went to him and offered him a coin. 'But he turned out to be not so poor, after all,' she recalls. 'He smiled sadly and would not take it. I can't describe my emotions; here was this man I wanted to comfort and console, and instead of that I had injured his feelings. I dare say the poor cripple guessed what was passing through my mind, because he turned back to smile at me.' She resolved then to remember to pray for that man when she made her First Holy Communion – 'I had been told that any prayer you said on that day would be granted' – and five years later, she kept that promise, 'and I hope that prayer was answered, a prayer God himself had inspired, a prayer for one of his suffering members.'

While recording such spiritual milestones as her First Confession – usually made at that time some years before the reception of First Holy Communion – and the Corpus Christi procession at which she delighted to throw petals 'even as high as the monstrance itself', and how the first sermon she understood was a moving one on the passion of Our Lord, Thérèse does not present a picture of a child saint. She gives some evidence that her relations with the nursery maid, Victoire, were not always amicable. On a May evening, when the rest of the family had gone to the May devotions but she was considered too young to go, she had made a little May altar of her own. Victoire, helping her, teased her playfully by pretending that she had forgotten some lights, and paid for her teasing when Thérèse called her a naughty girl and kicked her! As was her practice, she repented at once and tearfully resolved 'never to do it again'. She records how Victoire came to her aid on the occasion when, just as the maid was passing beside her with a bucket of water, she fell off a chair on which she had been balancing and landed in the bucket 'where I remained with my feet touching my head, fitting in as neatly as a chicken in its egg!' Another time, Thérèse fell into the fireplace, 'But fortunately the fire wasn't lit; so, Victoire had only to pick me up and shake the cinders off me.'

An incident that called for intervention from big sister, Marie, was caused by Victoire's refusal to fetch an ink-pot from the mantelpiece when requested to do so by Thérèse, too small to reach it. The maid, perhaps busy at the time, told her to get up on a chair and get the ink-pot herself. Thérèse did so, 'but it did seem to me,' she narrates, 'that it wasn't very nice of her, and by way of making that clear, I fished about in my childish vocabulary for the most offensive word I knew. When she was annoyed with me, she often called me 'a little brat', which I found very hurtful. So, before I got down off the chair, I turned round with a dignified air and said: "Victoire, you're a brat!" Then I ran for cover, leaving her to digest this deep insult.' (Lovers of Shakespeare will recall, perhaps, the retort of the savage, Caliban, to his sophisticated master, Prospero, in *The Tempest*: 'You have taught me language, and my profit on't is, I know how to curse'). The furious Victoire called out to authority in an adjacent room, 'Miss Marie, here's Thérèse been calling me a brat!' Even if Marie had known the whole story, she could not approve her young sister's behaviour and language; she ordered Thérèse to apologise, 'which I did,' says the narrator, 'but without being really sorry. If Victoire wouldn't even stretch out her great long arm to oblige me, what else would you call her?' Then, before anyone might suggest alternatives, Sister Thérèse spreads the light of holy charity on the episode: 'All the same, we were very fond of one another.'

Although Thérèse says that her father and sisters were careful to correct her when necessary and not to spoil her, it would have been difficult for them not to treat her with special love and care in view not only of her being the baby of the family but because of the tragic loss of her mother when she was still a child. Outside of the family circle, they tried to protect her from what they considered harmful compliments about her good looks or qualities. Thérèse recalls her first visit to the seaside when she was about eight years old. Her rhapsodic account of the beauty and majesty of the sea, as well as the spiritual connotation she establishes in her mature recollection of it, also includes the tale of how, as she played on the beach near her father, an elegant couple approached him to ask if that pretty little girl was his daughter. 'I noticed,' she writes, 'that Papa, as he said Yes, made a sign to show that he didn't want them to pay me compliments.'

Louis called her his little princess, and if the priest at Mass should happen to refer to St Teresa of Avila, he would lean over to her and whisper: 'Listen carefully, princess; this is about your patron saint.' She reciprocated by installing him as 'king of France and Navarre' in her imagination. 'I simply can't explain how fond I was of Papa,' she says to Pauline and the other sisters who will probably, she knows, read her manuscript. 'Sometimes he used to tell me his ideas about things in general, just as if I'd been a big girl; and I used to say, in my innocence, that if he put all that to the important government people, they'd be certain to take him and make a king of him, and then France would be happier than she'd ever been.' She then adds a precocious *caveat*: 'But if he'd been made King of France and Navarre, he'd certainly have been unhappy – all kings were.'

The only truly dark cloud to be found in Thérèse's sunny account of those four years between the family's arrival at Lisieux and her beginning formal school at the age of eight and a half is in her account of an incident concerning her father – or someone she believed to be him. She was just over six years old at the time, and Louis had been away from home for some days and was not due back for another two days. Thérèse, standing at a window overlooking the large garden behind the house, saw a man dressed exactly like her father, even to the same type of hat, and of his build and walk, except that he seemed much more bent or stooped. She did not see the man's face because it was muffled in a dark veil. Although she was convinced that it was her father, who had probably come home early and was muffled up because he wanted to surprise the family, she felt strangely disturbed instead of happy. She called out, 'Father! Father!' but the man walked steadily on and disappeared into a small clump of trees. Thérèse waited anxiously to see him come out on the other side, but he did not re-appear.

Her two eldest sisters, Marie and Pauline, were in the next room and heard her cries. Marie told her later that she herself felt a shock of terror on hearing them, but she did not let her young sister know this at the time. The older girls rushed in and asked why Thérèse was calling her father when they all knew he was in Alençon and would not be back home for some days more. When this did not calm her, they said it was probably the maid, Victoire, she had seen going about with her apron over her head to frighten some children. But Victoire was discovered in the kitchen and said she had not gone outside. Then the older girls took Thérèse with them down to the grove of trees, but found no trace of anyone in that area. They told her not to think about it any more; but she remained troubled about what she had seen, convinced that there was some meaning in it that she would learn later. Fourteen years later, not only Thérèse, but all the family were to endure the tragedy of seeing their father, who had always been so fine a specimen of manhood and culture in their eyes, afflicted in a manner that metamorphosed him into a pitiful shell of the remarkable man who had loved and cared for them. That tragedy was still mercifully hidden in the mists of the future. A more immediate and personal disruption was to occur in Thérèse's life when it was decided that she was now, at over eight years of age, ready to be enrolled at the local Benedictine school where Léonie had just finished and Céline was already a pupil. It was the real end of her childhood.

CHAPTER SIX

Unwillingly to School

'I've often heard it said,' Sister Thérèse muses, 'that one's schooldays are the best and the happiest days of one's life; but I can't say I found them so. I have never been so melancholy as I was during those five years.' As usual, she compares herself to a little flower, this time as one transplanted from a special soil of its own to a common garden where it must contend for survival with others of many varieties. Her problem was two-fold, the one social, the other intellectual. She had lived up to now in a protected family environment of piety and culture, and she had been educated by her sisters, Marie and Pauline, to a standard far above that of other girls of her age. Now, although first in her class and praised by the teachers, she found herself envied and bullied by some of her much older classmates; the situation was not helped by the nuns' sympathetic petting of her as the little orphan daughter of the highly-respected Monsieur Louis Martin.

Although Céline, four years older, tried to defend her sister against taunts and bullying in the playground – 'Only for Céline was in the school with me,' she says, 'I would not have been able to stand it' – the family were not aware of the situation or its effect on Thérèse. From an early age, she had been inculcated by her parents and sisters into the pious attitude of regarding trouble and problems as an opportunity for self-sacrifice, and she had resolved never to complain about anything. All her doting father knew about her days at school was when she came home in the evening, sat on his knee, and told him about her achievements in class. He would reward her weekly with a coin which she put away in a money-box; this box, in turn, became the source of her personal contributions on feast days to the Society for the Propagation of the Faith and other such charities. The three older girls were also in the dark about Thérèse's problems at school.

Even when she and Céline met with their two Guérin cousins, Jeanne and Marie, every Thursday afternoon, Thérèse disliked the organised games and dance practice. For Marie Guérin and herself – 'we were twin souls, we always had the same instincts' – she devised a game her schoolmates would certainly have derided: they were to be two hermits, with a little hut and a small garden, living the contemplative life, one working while the other prayed. When Marie's mother sent them out for a walk with the two older girls, they continued to be 'hermits', saying the rosary on their fingers. They carried their game too far one day when they decided that hermits should walk along the street with their eyes closed so as not to be distracted. Inevitably, they knocked over some boxes of goods outside a shop. The shopkeeper's anger and their sisters' embarrassment put an end to the game of hermits.

The older girls punished them by separating them on future walks, Thérèse having to walk with Jeanne Guérin, Céline with Marie Guérin. Sister Thérèse concludes this quaint reminiscence with the shrewd observation: 'This put an end to our fatal unanimity, and it wasn't a bad thing for the two elder ones either, because they weren't twin souls at all, they used to argue all the way home.' If that irate shopkeeper in Lisieux had been a prophet, he might have told the two giddy little hermits that Marie Guérin would enter Carmel in 1895, just two years before the death of Sister Thérèse of the Child Jesus, and be one of the small group of novices, including Thérèse's own sister, Céline, who would be able to thank God for the rest of their religious lives that they had had a saint as their novice-mistress.

At home, Thérèse continued to learn from her sisters, especially now from Céline who was able to pass on the formal school teaching. Like many children, Céline played a game of 'school', her dolls as pupils, herself as teacher, and Thérèse as assistant or parent as required. When Pauline began to prepare Céline for her First Holy Communion, Thérèse was a silent observer, as usual adding to her precocious knowledge while dreaming of how her own turn would come to have similar instruction from the beloved big sister she regarded as a surrogate mother. That dream was shattered when Pauline told her father that she had decided to enter the Carmelite convent in Lisieux. What made the shock even more severe was that Thérèse had not been told of this before she happened to overhear Pauline discussing her decision with the eldest sister, Marie.

As a child of four, Thérèse had heard people saying that Pauline would surely become a nun. Although too young to understand, she told Pauline that she wanted to go with her to a far-off desert where they could both be nuns. The big sister playfully said they would have to wait until Thérèse was old enough. Thérèse was now old enough to know what a nun was, although not quite clear as to what the enclosed life at Carmel implied. She knew that Pauline was leaving the family to go into a convent; so, having lost her real mother when only a child, she was now to lose her second 'mother'. Although she did not consciously count as a mother the countrywoman, Rose Taillé, who had lovingly nursed her back to health as a baby, this would be, in effect, the third time she was to suffer the disruption and loss involved in such a separation. 'I can't tell you what misery I went through at that moment,' Thérèse tells Pauline in her manuscript recollections. But the shock news also helped the process of maturing, for she adds: 'This was life, I told myself, life, that up to this had not seemed so bad. Life, when you saw it as it really was, just meant continual suffering, continual separation.' Then Sister Thérèse takes over the pen: 'I cried bitterly over it, having no idea yet of the joy that comes from sacrifice.'

Her father had his own loss and sorrow to contend with as a result of Pauline's decision, although it cannot have been a very great shock to so devout a man that one of his daughters, brought up in such a pious family, should become a nun; also, Pauline must have been in touch with the nuns in Carmel for some time (whether the two eldest girls had some social life in Lisieux, perhaps even some proposals of marriage, is naturally a topic not touched on in the conventual writings of their youngest sister). It was left to Pauline herself to try to console young Thérèse. This she did by pointing out that the family would be able to visit her in the convent; but she also described the life of the nuns in Carmel with such enthusiasm and in such glowing spiritual terms that Thérèse began to see it as the secluded holy place she used to envisage in which God meant her to go and live. She was old enough now, at nine, to analyse the spiritual intimations in her own soul of these religious developments in the family.

Listening to Pauline's analysis of her own vocation, Thérèse came to the conclusion that God was calling her also to the religious life. 'So strong was my feeling about this,' she writes, 'that it left no shadow of doubt on my mind; it wasn't just the dream of an impressionable child, it was certain with all the certainty of a divine vocation. I didn't want to go into Carmel for Pauline's sake, but for our Lord's sake and no other reason. Words won't do justice to all that was in my mind, but now I was completely at rest.'

Next day, Thérèse took Pauline into her confidence and Pauline promised to take her to visit Carmel so that she could talk to the Mother Prioress about her desire to be a nun 'for our Lord's sake and no other reason'. Thérèse, of course, had already mapped out the course of events in her determined mind – she could enter Carmel with Pauline and make her First Holy Communion the day Pauline was clothed with the habit. She even had given deep thought to the name she would have as a nun, and decided, because of her devotion to the Child Jesus, that she would keep her own name, 'such a lovely name', and add on that of the Child Jesus.

On the Sunday appointed for the visit, Thérèse met for the first time the aristocratic and cultured Mother Marie de Gonzague who, while agreeing that Thérèse's desire seemed to be the sign of a true vocation, had to point out gently that the

Carmelites could not accept a girl of nine as a postulant; she would have to wait until she was sixteen. It was of some consolation to the would-be postulant to learn that, in discussion with the other nuns, Mother de Gonzague had already settled on a name in religion for her, none other than Sister Thérèse of the Child Jesus. It looks as though Pauline may have had a private word with the Prioress on that matter.

Although she could now live with the hope of some day being reunited with Pauline in Carmel, and the family could visit every Thursday, Thérèse still felt the emotional wrench of separation when Pauline entered Carmel in October of that year. Pauline had been her tutor and confidante, her guide and exemplar. Without telling tales or complaining about her troubles at school, she had found consolation and relief on returning home every evening to the maternal care lavished on her by the big sister she had chosen to replace her beloved mother. Now she could see Pauline for only a brief period once a week, and then only in the company of the whole family. An incident remembered by the eldest sister, Marie (Sister Marie of the Sacred Heart), reveals the pathetic plight in which Thérèse found herself during those family visits.

> One day, when nobody was paying very much attention to her, Thérèse said quietly, 'Look, Pauline, I'm wearing the little skirt you made for me.' 'But,' Marie admits candidly, 'I went on talking and nobody took any notice of Thérèse.'

Another instance of Marie's unintentional but damaging treatment of her youngest sister was recorded later by Céline. When their Father, impressed by the artistic talent of Céline, offered to get her lessons from a private tutor, Thérèse, as always, was on hand to hear. Céline saw from her face that she wanted to be included in the lessons; so did Louis himself, but when he put the question to Thérèse, Marie interrupted, saying it would be a waste of money as Thérèse did not have the same talent and also that the house was already cluttered up with 'smearings that had to be framed'. Marie, of course, must have been weary at times, now that she had the full care of the house and the management of the maids, as well as the supervision of the younger children. She was soon called on to show the genuine love she undoubtedly had for Thérèse.

The daily troubles at school, combined with the parting from Pauline, brought on an illness that almost proved fatal to Thérèse and threw the family and their relatives into turmoil. At Easter in 1883 Louis took Marie and Léonie to Paris, leaving Céline and Thérèse in the safe and loving care of their Uncle Isidore Guérin and his wife. Uncle Isidore, however, did not have a high opinion of Thérèse's character – he considered her withdrawn, sentimenal and too prone to tears and worry. One day, when he took her for a walk, he began to reminisce about her mother, his own sister, Zélie. Thérèse, too, had her memories of a loving mother, and she had recently lost her replacement, Pauline. She broke down in tears, much to the annoyance of Uncle Isidore. He decided that what she and her sister, Céline, needed was some social contact and excitement. At home, he announced that he would bring them, along with his own two daughters, to the Catholic Social Club that very evening, where they could enjoy dancing, music and pleasant company. He did not realise that he was giving a very traumatised young girl a final emotional push into breakdown.

For some months before this, Thérèse had been suffering from continual headaches, but 'I went on with my school work and nobody was worried about me.' Just as they were about to set off for the Club, Thérèse became ill. Her Aunt Céline put her to bed while the others went on to enjoy the social evening. The doctor was called next day, but he was mystified by the illness. Louis and the two older girls were recalled from Paris and were horrified to find Thérèse seemingly at death's door. Marie stayed on at the Guérin house to care for Thérèse who recovered sufficiently to be able to attend, with all the rest of the family, at the ceremony in Carmel on the day Pauline was clothed. Next day, however, back at home at *Les Buissonets*, Thérèse was ill again, even worse than she had been. This mysterious illness lasted for a few months, during which time she was often delirious and hallucinating, sometimes seeming paralysed, but yet aware of what was being done and said all around her. Later, she would ascribe it to the devil, angry at the entry of Pauline into Carmel and 'determined to get revenge on us for all the loss of influence our family was to involve him in; but if Almighty God allowed the devil to come very close,' she wrote, 'he also sent me angels in visible form.' These ministering angels were her father and her three sisters, especially Marie – 'Poor Marie, what she went through, what unselfish care she lavished on me! I can never be grateful enough.'

The family's worry was shared by Pauline and the nuns in Carmel. Pauline added to the prayers being said by sending a letter to Thérèse along with a doll dressed up as a Carmelite, a present that evoked contrary reactions. The outspoken Uncle Isidore disapproved, saying it would be much better to make the patient forget about Carmel, while Thérèse herself was naturally pleased – 'My own feeling was that the hope of being a Carmelite one day was the only thing that was keeping me alive.' Marie had installed Thérèse in her own bedroom, where they had also placed the statue of Our Lady which had originally stood in the garden of Louis' private Pavilion at Alençon and had later been the focus of family prayers as it was now at *Les Buissonets*. To this revered statue, Thérèse says, 'I often turned my head in silent prayer, like a flower that turns its head towards the sun.' One day, she saw her grieving father giving some gold coins to Marie, and heard that it was for the purpose of having a novena of Masses offered for her recovery at Our Lady of Victories church in Paris. It was while that novena of Masses was still in progress that Thérèse was cured, instantaneously and, as she and the family believed, miraculously.

One Sunday morning, while Marie was in the garden and Léonie was reading near the window in the bedroom, Thérèse began to call out 'Mamma! Mamma!', at first in a whisper, then louder. Léonie summoned Marie and Céline, but Thérèse did not recognise them and went on calling 'Mamma!' The girls became alarmed and knelt before the statue in desperation to ask Our Lady's help for their sister. Thérèse writes: 'I, too, had turned towards the statue, and all my heart went into a prayer that my Mother in heaven would have pity on me. All at once, she let me see her in her beauty, a beauty that surpassed all my experience – her face wore such a look of kindness and pity as I cannot describe; but what pierced me to the heart was her smile. With that, all my distress came to an end.'

While feeling that her health had been instantly restored, Thérèse also sensed that she should keep secret what she had seen. 'I mustn't tell anybody about it; if I did, my happiness would disappear.' But her sister Marie, observing her, had noticed the change in her features while gazing at the statue and she began to surmise that something strange had taken place. She gave her own account of the incident in later testimony: 'I saw Thérèse all of a sudden staring at the statue; her look was radiant. I understood she was restored, that she was looking not at the image of Mary but at the Blessed Virgin herself. She remained in ecstasy for four or five minutes.'

Marie cried out, 'Thérèse is cured!' As soon as she was alone with her young sister, she began to probe, asking what was it Thérèse had seen. Because of the loving care Marie had lavished on her all during her illness, and perhaps because she was still weak and tired, Thérèse felt that she could not refuse 'such loving, eager inquiries as hers'. Not only did she tell Marie, 'as simply and openly as I could', all that she had experienced, but she also agreed when Marie asked her permission to pass on the story to Pauline and the nuns in Carmel. On her next visit to Carmel, Thérèse had the joy of seeing Pauline in the Carmelite habit, but that joy soon evaporated when Mother Gonzague and other nuns gathered round her to question her about what all were now convinced had been a miraculous healing through the intercession of Our Blessed Lady. The eager nuns wanted to know if the Blessed Virgin was carrying the Child Jesus in her arms? Was there a great blaze of light? And so on. Thérèse, confused and unhappy, could only repeat: 'The Blessed Virgin looked very beautiful, and I saw her smile down at me.'

What had been a mystical experience of spiritual joy and physical healing now became for the young Thérèse a source of mental torment. 'My instinct had been all too true,' she writes, 'because from then on my happiness disappeared, and I regretted bitterly what I'd done. For four years the memory of that wonderful grace I'd received was a real torment to me … For a long time after I got well, I was convinced that I had made myself ill on purpose.' She discussed her scruples with Marie, and later with her confessor, both of them assuring her that she could not possibly have wished herself into so serious and alarming an illness. As usual, with the analytic spiritual hindsight of her final years of life, Sister Thérèse interprets the unpleasant consequences of her sisterly revelation as a step in her path towards holiness. 'I suppose,' she surmises, 'Almighty God meant to purify and above all to humble me, so he allowed this secret torment of mine to go on right up to the time when I entered Carmel.' And again: 'I feel sure that if I had kept my secret, I could have kept my peace of mind; as it was, Our Lady allowed this trial to befall me, for my soul's good; without it, I might have given way to vanity, instead of accepting humiliation as my lot.' Her conclusion, however, reveals that the mental and spiritual torment of the scruples she endured for years afterwards must have been a more severe affliction than the actual illness of which they were the unexpected consequence. In a sentence brief but chilling, she says: 'But what suffering it brought me – I shall never be able to describe it, not in this world.'

CHAPTER SEVEN

The Little Doctor

A few months after her recovery, Thérèse revisited the scenes of her childhood in Alençon for the first time since coming to live in Lisieux. Louis took the family there for a fortnight, during which they visited their mother's grave and renewed acquaintance with friends; we are not told whether they made contact with the family of Rose Taillé, but it is likely that they made the trip to the farm or arranged a meeting in the town. Although Thérèse was just ten years old, she was already fully resolved to become a Carmelite nun; not surprisingly, therefore, her impressions of the worldly people, as she calls them, whom they met in Alençon, people 'who had the knack of serving God and at the same time enjoying, to the full, the good things of earth', are influenced by that mindset. She admits, however, to the attraction that kind of life exercises, and considers it a great grace that she experienced it for only a short while.

Back at school, Thérese sought relief from its daily unpleasantnesses by spending more of her home time in reading. 'I could have spent a whole lifetime in reading,' she says. 'This love of reading stayed with me right up to the time when I entered Carmel. I couldn't possibly reckon up the number of books that passed through my hands.' Although she admits to having read some romantic tales 'which made me forget, at the time, the realities of life,' her books, of course, were carefully chosen for her, so that 'I never read a single one that could be harmful to me.' Her favoured reading was about 'heroic Frenchwomen, like the Venerable Jeanne d'Arc, who loved their country so well.' Little did she realise that only five years would separate the canonisation of St Jeanne d'Arc in 1920 from that of St Thérèse of the Child Jesus in 1925, and that, in 1944 Pope Pius

XII would name her co-patron of France with the heroine of her childhood. She did feel inspired, however, to emulate Jeanne and other such figures.

'I felt that I was born for greatness,' she says candidly; but adds, 'When I asked myself how I was to achieve it, God put into my mind … the glory which was reserved for me was one which didn't reveal itself to human eyes; I must devote myself to becoming a great saint.' Again analysing her youthful sentiments, Sister Thérèse distinguishes between the possible conceit inherent in such an ambition and the humility with which a soul so inspired by God lays itself open to whatever suffering may be required in following the path of sanctity with the aid of God's grace. She was indeed destined, through a life of prayer, sacrifice and suffering, to become a great saint, but she was mistaken in thinking that if she did so, the glory of that achievement would be kept hidden by God from the eyes of the world.

Although Thérèse had made her First Confession some years before this, she was only now, as was the custom of that time, about to receive her First Holy Communion. While Marie took on the instruction in the home, Pauline joined in from Carmel by sending Thérèse a special treatise about the sacrament and also by writing her a weekly letter. It was the practice also that the girls preparing for First Communion spend three days in retreat as boarders in the Benedictine school. The separation involved in this was not very penitential – her father and sisters visited her every day; also, the nuns, probably mindful of her recent severe illness, petted her with maternal care, even sending her to the infirmary one morning because she had a cough. The same nuns were surprised, and perhaps amused, when they found that this eleven-year-old girl did not know how to dress herself or comb her hair – her older sisters had prolonged her childhood to that extent. They must also have been amused when, as she wryly admits, she made herself conspicuous by going about wearing in her belt a large crucifix – a present from Léonie, she recalls – such as missionaries wear. The nuns decided that she was probably trying to imitate her big sister in Carmel.

Spiritually, however, the retreat involved no such petting. The elderly priest conducting the retreat, Fr Domin, had been chaplain to the school for over forty years, and the talks he gave to young girls preparing for First Communion were more suited to the conversion of hardened sinners on the point of death. His theology and spirituality were of the jansenistic school, portraying God as a righteous but stern judge, while also stressing the difficulty of avoiding sin, and the eternal damnation in the fires of hell awaiting even young people who were not constantly on their guard against the snares of the devil. This was not the loving and merciful God in whom Thérèse had been learning to confide, and towards whom, in the image of his humanity as the Child Jesus, and herself as a little flower he might pick, she had already begun to direct the spirituality that was later to blossom into a mystical love of God like that of her patron, St Teresa of Avila, and her inspirational Carmelite poet, St John of the Cross. Sad to say, it was in that same jansenistic style that even younger children were prepared for First Holy Communion after Pope St Pius X lowered the age for its reception, and it was not until the Second Vatican Council midway through the twentieth century, over fifty years after her death, that the 'little way' of love for a loving God by which Thérèse had achieved sainthood began to permeate the theology of the church in general.

Although other sources tell us that she was distressed and even wept as a result of the chaplain's lectures, Thérèse herself says only, 'I listened attentively to the instruction which the Abbé Domin gave us, and made an abstract of them, though I didn't keep any record of my private meditations.' She adds that her general confession in preparation for First Communion 'left my soul utterly at peace; God didn't want any cloud to overshadow me.' She does record that the joy of receiving God into her soul at First Communion caused her to weep, much to the puzzlement of her companions, who ascribed her tears to the absence of her mother. Appropriately in view of his early years in the trade, her father presented her with a lovely watch to mark the occasion. Knowing who was likely to read her manuscript,

Thérèse does not feel it necessary to expatiate on the spiritual emotions evoked by her First Holy Communion: 'I don't want to go into detail ... There are experiences of the soul which you can't express without losing their inner meaning, their heavenly meaning.'

It was the custom then that the reception of First Communion, at about the age of twelve, was followed soon after by the sacrament of Confirmation. Her comments are again indicative of how her individualistic path of holiness was already developing. 'I could never understand why people didn't take more trouble about it, this sacrament which was all centred in love.' Remembering the events of Pentecost as recorded by Saint Luke in the Acts of the Apostles – 'all at once a sound came from heaven, like that of a strong wind blowing, and it filled the whole house' – she says, 'My experience when the Holy Spirit came to me was not that of a strong wind blowing; it was more like that "whisper of a gentle breeze" which Elias heard on Mount Horeb.' But she concludes, ominously, 'I was granted, that day, the strength to suffer; the ordeal was to begin.'

The ordeal was caused by another dose of the sermons of Fr Domin, in preparation for Confirmation. Thérèse, now aged twelve and a half, lost her confidence in her own loving attitude to God. She became totally obsessed with scruples about the state of her own soul, unsure of her relationship with God, fearing that her thoughts and actions might be sinful in some way known to God but not to her. She did not mention this mental and spiritual torment to her father, but confided in her sister, Marie. In spite of Marie's wise counsel, Thérèse was still suffering the agony of scruples a year and a half later when Marie followed Pauline into Carmel. Then, 'having lost my earthly confidante,' she says, I could only have recourse to heaven.' Strangely, she chose to pray, not to her Mother, but to the four children of the family who had died in infancy or early childhood. She told them candidly that she, as the youngest, had always been spoilt, and that they also, had they lived, would have been just as kind to her as her four living siblings had been. 'Now, with all the resources of heaven at their disposal, they could easily win me the peace of mind I wanted, and prove that love doesn't end with death.' Very soon, her scruples vanished completely and 'a delicious sense of peace flooded into my soul'. She continued ever after to pray to 'those four innocent souls that had made their way to heaven before me'.

Before that cure and the departure of Marie for Carmel, Thérèse had had to face back to school after her Confirmation. She was still loath to join in games – 'I was often to be found leaning up against a tree and indulging in serious thought' – but she was also anxious to make friends and please people. She devised ways of doing so, one of them original in a macabre sense. She began to bury, apparently with some ostentatious ceremony, 'the little birds that we found lying dead under the trees'. Other girls joined in this sentimental pastime, and soon they had established a little cemetery decorated with tree-shoots and tiny flowers 'to match the size of our feathered friends'.

Thérèse, more of a reader than the others, had another resource in her efforts to be accepted. She began telling stories to little groups, stories she composed as she went along and that sometimes lasted from day to day – a storyteller's device that stretches as far back as Scheherezade and *The Thousand and One Nights*, that also proved profitable to Charles Dickens when he published his novels first as magazine serials, and that constitutes the main requirement in the unfortunate talented hacks who, in our own day, have to earn their bread by concocting television soap operas. This unusual schoolyard entertainment being provided by the young loner, Mlle Martin, began to attract even some of the senior girls. At which point, probably, authority stepped in when a mistress broke up the circle with the comment that 'playtime was intended to exercise the pupils' muscles and not their brains'.

In the classroom, Thérèse continued to impress, even to the extent of being called his 'little Doctor' by old Fr Domin – in reference to her patron, the 'great' doctor, Teresa of Avila – because of her knowledge of the Cathechism and the Bible; but even this success was soured on occasion when her frustration at not gaining first place issued in tears. She does not mention in her manuscripts whether she actually put forward in religion class the views she expressed elsewhere, in correspondence and conversation; if she did, that hellfire preacher must have been surprised and perhaps perturbed to hear a girl of thirteen offer her belief in a loving God as a better means to salvation than his traditional hellfire teaching, and suggest that Holy Communion should be received frequently, even daily, rather than rarely as was the current custom when one had to ask permission of one's confessor. 'I made a rule of receiving Holy Communion as often as my confessor would let me,' writes Sister Thérèse, 'but allowing him to judge for himself, not asking it of him as a favour. Nowadays,' she adds, 'I should be braver, and take the opposite view ... After all, our Lord doesn't come down from heaven every day just to wait there in a gold ciborium; he has found a much better heaven for his resting-place, a Christian soul, made in his own image, the living temple of the Blessed Trinity.'

Deserving of special notice is her thought concerning the current and long-lasting teaching of the church, imputed to the influence of St Augustine, that babies who died without baptism did not go to heaven but to a place of peace and rest called Limbo. In her First Communion class, when some of the girls found some malicious light relief from Fr Domin's sermons by jokingly naming some of the people likely to go to hell, Thérèse maintained that if she were God she would save them all. Her attitude to the teaching on Limbo was similar; she considered that, God being almighty, he would have no problem with bringing unbaptised infants to heaven.

If the theologians in Rome had only consulted that young girl in a school in Lisieux, and adopted her views then, they would have saved many unfortunate Catholic mothers deep and lasting distress. It took another half-century, and the prolonged theological discussions of the Second Vatican Council, before Limbo was deleted from the catechism. The very name is not to be found in the index or the text of the official *Catechism of the*

Catholic Church published in 1994 – fifty years after Vatican Two; but, in the section on baptism, the hair-splitting theologians go so far as to say, with some italics (VI, 1261): 'As regards children *who have died without baptism*, the church can only entrust them to the mercy of God, as she does in her funeral rites for them. Indeed, the great mercy of God who desires that all men should be saved, and Jesus' tenderness towards children which caused him to say: "Let the children come to me, do not hinder them," allow us to hope that there is a way of salvation for children who have died without baptism.' One doubts if that would have satisfied young Thérèse Martin, or even Sister Thérèse of the Child Jesus, or if it would now satisfy Saint Thérèse whom one could imagine being asked by God to take charge of a special nursery in heaven for those special Holy Innocents.

CHAPTER EIGHT

An End to Childhood

Back on earth in the town of Lisieux in the year 1886, events were developing which would bring about the ending of Thérèse's prolonged childhood and her sudden alteration into the mentally mature and determined girl who would overcome all obstacles in order to fulfil her vocation to Carmel. While her education at home and in school, aided by her avid reading – she had also begun to study science and history on her own – had made her intellectually far advanced beyond her years, Thérèse was still being treated as the baby of the family by her father and her sisters. She had taken over an attic room, used previously by Céline for her painting, and her description of the variety of objects she packed into it makes it sound like the imagined magic world of a child. One item was 'a cage with a lot of birds in it', and she comments, 'their chirping made visitors put their hands to their ears'. For a young girl who sentimentally buried dead birds in a corner of the school playground, to keep live birds, including a linnet and a canary, in a cage seems some-how out of character; but then, her father, Louis had given her, at different ages, presents of a magpie, a dog, and a lamb. One can only say, as he might, *autres temps, autres moeurs.*

Outside that close domestic scene where she continued to be petted and protected, and enjoyed the prolongation of that loving treatment, opinions on Thérèse varied. As we have seen, her blunt Uncle Isidore, not realising her inhibitions in his presence, considered her weak in character, childishly sentimental, and not very bright; on the other hand, her teachers, even the formidable Fr Domin, with experience only of her intellectual qualities and book learning, considered her precocious and educated beyond her years. Thérèse recalls how one of the mistresses at the Abbey asked her one day what she did with herself on holidays when left to her own devices. 'I told her that I got behind my bed, where there was an empty space in which you could shut yourself away with the curtains, and there, well, there I used to think.' 'Think about what?' the nun asked. 'Oh, about God, and about life, and eternity; *you* know, I just think.' (the stress on the word *you* is by the pen of Sister Thérèse). 'The dear nun,' she continues, tongue in cheek, 'made a great joke of this, and later on used to remind me of my thinking days, and ask me whether I still thought.' Sister Thérèse was too charitable to comment that the 'dear nun' seemingly had forgotten that plaintive voice calling to humanity from the pages of the Old Testament: 'With desolation is the whole world made desolate, because there is no one who thinks in his heart.'

As a young teenager, Thérèse's life was further complicated by her physical development and the incipient awareness of sexuality. Without a mother since she was four, she was soon to be deprived of the last substitute in the form of her eldest sister, Marie. She became disturbed and ill again when her sister, Céline, finished her schooling at the Benedictines. Her cousin, Marie Guérin, had also left. After six months, Louis decided to take Thérèse from the school and have her continue her education with a private teacher, Madame Papinau, who had been giving lessons to Pauline. This lady lived with her aged mother, and a cat, and the lessons were often interrupted by visitors whose gushing comments on the attractive young pupil were privately interpreted by that same pupil as further evidence of the folly of the world.

When their father, Louis, went on a tour as far as Constantinople, now Istanbul, with a local curate and some others, Marie sent the two younger girls for a seaside holiday with the Guérins. Although their aunt, Céline Guérin, did her best to make the holiday enjoyable – 'she gave us all the treats she could think of, donkey-rides and shrimping and so on' – an incident during that holiday helped in the process of maturing self-awareness for Thérèse and caused her to deprecate herself as being no better than those donkeys she rode at the beach.

Her cousin, Marie Guérin, suffering from chronic headaches, cried constantly and was petted by her loving mother. Thérèse had suffered from headaches for years, but had taken a pious resolution not to complain about that or anything else unpleasant in life; now, however, perhaps envying the maternal love being lavished on her cousin, Thérèse decided she would like to share in some of that attention. She sat on an armchair and burst into tears, explaining that she had a headache, which was true; but her aunt and her older cousin, Jeanne, decided that there must be some other reason for her tears; so, instead of sympathy and petting she got a scolding.

'Well,' she comments, 'I had bought my experience cheap; no more imitating other people for me. I understood now the fable about the donkey and the pet dog.' For those who have suffered the tragedy of forgetting their fairy tales and fables, a reminder: the donkey in Aesop's fable – probably read by Thérèse in the rhyming French version by La Fontaine – comparing his lot as a beast of burden, enduring blows and insults, with that of the pet dog who, greeting the master with noisy yelps and jumps, was rewarded with petting, good food, and a place by the fire, decided to do likewise; but his master, alarmed when the hitherto placid beast suddenly jumped at him with deafening hee-haws, responded by driving him off with even heavier blows than normal.

When Louis Martin returned from his tour of foreign parts he suffered a shock so severe as to cancel any pleasure he had derived from his trip. His eldest daughter, Marie, now twenty-six, announced that she had decided to follow Pauline into Carmel. During the years of his happy married life, Louis had often heard his wife, Zélie, express the devout wish, not only that she might have a son a priest, but that all her children would be called to dedicate their lives, in religious orders, to the service of God and the welfare of humanity. As his five daughters grew up, it was Pauline, the second eldest, who first showed signs of fulfilling their dead mother's wish; consequently, when, at twenty-one, she decided to enter Carmel, it did not come as any great surprise to the devout widower. However, since his wife's death and the family's move to Lisieux, Louis had come to regard Marie, his eldest daughter, as settled into the role of efficient housekeeper and genuinely happy to be the maternal mentor and tutor of the younger girls. She had hitherto, as far as he knew, shown no inclination to the religious life, and if any offers of marriage had come her way she had obviously refused them for whatever reason. Now, five years after Pauline's entry, that Marie should decide to leave him and the three remaining children and follow her sister to Carmel was undoubtedly a severe shock to the ageing father. In retrospect, he may have considered that Marie's decision was influenced by a Jesuit priest who was her spiritual adviser and also a family friend. It is recorded that Louis, torn by conflicting emotions, looked at his daughter with tears in his eyes and said, 'God could not have asked a greater sacrifice from me. I thought you would never leave me!'

Being the devout man he was, however, Louis Martin made that sacrifice, as he was to make more of the same. He gave Marie his blessing on her vocation, but also decided to take her on a last visit to her birthplace at Alençon so that she could say farewell to relatives and the friends of her childhood. He also brought the other three daughters, Léonie, now aged twenty-three, Céline, aged eighteen, and Thérèse, aged fourteen. It was Léonie, the middle one of his five daughters and the one who had given most concern by her moods as an adolescent, who now inflicted a further shock on the devoted father, a man already trying to cope with the mental anguish of parting with Marie. One day, Léonie went off on her own to the Convent of the Poor Clares in Alençon where she told the Reverend Mother that she wished to enter the order. Surprisingly – unless there had been some previous correspondence unknown to her father – the young woman was encouraged by the Reverend Mother to join up at once. Thérèse records 'the embarrassment and the kindness with which Papa broke the news' to Marie and the two younger girls. 'He was as much surprised as we were,' she adds, 'but he didn't like to say so, because he could see that Marie was taking it badly.' Marie's displeasure was caused by the fact that she was due to enter Carmel in a week's time, and she had assumed that Léonie would gladly take over her role in the family home. Now that duty would have to fall on the next-in-line, the eighteen-year-old Céline.

When Louis was made aware that Léonie had stayed on as a postulant in the Poor Clare Convent, the astonished father must have hastened to the convent in some distress to discuss his daughter's decision, and that of the Reverend Mother, with both parties. If he had any qualms about the situation, his state of shock would have caused him not to enter into argument with Léonie, now a young woman of twenty-three, who had always been unpredictable. He obviously decided sadly to leave the matter in God's hands. Before returning to Lisieux, however, he brought the other girls to say farewell to Léonie (it is not clear from Thérèse's account whether the disgruntled Marie came along). 'When we went round to the convent,' she writes, 'it gave me a stifled sort of feeling I'd never had anywhere else: it wasn't a bit like Carmel, where your heart went out to everything you saw; the nuns, too, didn't attract me, and I wasn't in the least tempted to stay there.' Far be it from a poor common sinner like the present author to suggest a touch of conventual bias in all that, but while it might make for pleasant reading to the nuns in Carmel, it probably caused some caustic comment in the community rooms of Poor Clare convents years later when *The Story of a Soul* began to circulate in book form.

Both Marie in Carmel and her father in *Les Buissonets* must have felt more human relief than spiritual disappointment when Léonie returned home in less than two months, the régime of the Poor Clares proving too much for her health or her liking. The twin experience of seeing Marie enter Carmel and Léonie return from the Poor Clares caused the mind of Thérèse to concentrate even more on her own vocation to Carmel and to prepare for this by making special efforts to please God. But, as she acknowledges in her own account, she was still immature and childishly sensitive even at fourteen years of age. Although 'burning with desire to do good,' she says, 'I set about it in a very odd way.' She gives an example: 'Being the youngest, I had never learned to look after myself; it was Céline who made both beds in the room we slept in, and I never did anything.' She decided now that she would 'make the bed sometimes'. However, when she had done this great deed, or others of the kind, and they were not noticed and praised, she felt miserable and burst into tears. The same emotional result followed when she thought she had offended or annoyed anyone. With the precocious side of her mind, she then analysed this reaction and wept in disappointment because she had wept! All of this inner conflict caused her to realise, as she looked back on those days of frustration, that something drastic was needed to jolt her from her prolonged childhood into the maturity necessary for her future well-being. The event that caused this abrupt and traumatic transformation she sees in spiritual terms: 'God had to perform a miracle on a small scale to make me grow up.'

That this metamorphosis in the life of a teenage girl should be caused by what was just a casual remark made by her father would seem inexplicable to anyone who did not know the previous history of the relationship between Thérèse and the loving father whom she had adored since childhood. To him, she was always his 'little Princess', and she, even as a child, had given him the title 'King of France and Navarre' and believed him to be the only man good and wise enough to solve all the problems of the country. It was at Christmas 1866, a few months after Marie's entry into Carmel, when Louis and the three remaining girls returned from Midnight Mass, that the transforming 'miracle' took place that was to shake Thérèse into the awareness that she was not a child but a young woman, and should face the realities of life as such.

It was apparently the custom in families like the Martins that, on Christmas night, the children placed their slippers in the chimney corner, as children elsewhere hung a stocking over the fireplace; this they would later find mysteriously full of little presents. 'We had loved this so much in our childhood,' Thérèse writes, 'that Céline went on treating me as if I were a baby, as being the youngest. Papa was always so fond of seeing my happiness, and listening to my cries of delight as the magic slipper revealed, one after another, my surprise presents, and part of my happiness was the pleasure he took in it.' This Christmas night was the fateful occasion when that prolonged charade came to an end. While Thérèse was going upstairs to take off her hat, she overheard her father, as he noticed her slippers positioned, as usual, in the chimney corner, comment with a sigh of relief, 'Well, thank goodness, it's the last year this is going to happen!' It was as if the whole fabric of the fanciful king-princess relationship between them had suddenly been blown away. The stairs itself might have been a symbol of her instant painful progress from childish pretence to realistic truth.

Céline had also heard their weary father's instinctive reaction to the prospect of once again going through the childish charade of the slippers with his fourteen-year-old 'Princess', a prolongation of childhood in which they had both played their respective parts, and she knew what its effect could be on Thérèse. She hurried to console Thérèse, whom she expected to find in tears, and to advise her not to go downstairs just yet as she would only be miserable playing the game. She was astonished to find her young sister changed into what must have seemed a completely different person. Thérèse was obviously holding back tears, but she was also resolute and confident, determined to go down and take her part in the childish ritual with her father, albeit for the last time, without letting him see that he had unwittingly hurt her.

From that night on, however, Louis and her sisters saw clearly that Thérèse had finally left her childhood behind her and had blossomed suddenly into a mature and self-confident, but no less loving, young woman. Thérèse herself, more aware now, perhaps, of the deleterious effect on her of the loss of her mother, sums up the change in a sentence: 'Baby Thérèse had recovered the strength of mind which she'd lost at four and a half, and recovered it for good.' And she concludes: 'With this night of illumination, the third period of my life begins, the best of all, the richest in heavenly graces.' She now had a clear view both of herself and of what she intended to do with her life, and she set out with determination and humility, and with total confidence in God's grace, to fulfil what she saw as her destiny.

CHAPTER NINE

The Rocky Road to Carmel

One of the first results of the change in Thérèse's character was that her faith and piety became more outgoing and inclusive in her interpretation of life and humanity in general. She began to feel 'a great desire to work for the conversion of sinners,' a desire enhanced in her soul one day when she happened to come across one of her holy pictures, an image of Jesus on the Cross. Her poetic imagination fixed on the blood flowing from one of his nailed hands, and she decided that she would stand, in spirit, at the foot of the Cross, hearing our Lord's cry, 'I thirst', as an appeal for the salvation of sinners by means of this sacred blood. Through her prayers and sacrifices, she would gather the precious redeeming blood of Jesus and apply it to the souls of sinners.

With the restoration of her will-power and confidence since that event on Christmas night, Thérèse was now facing life with a more practical attitude than the sentimental and too sensitive girl she had been up to then; so, instead of being content with just feeling a desire to save sinners from damnation, she decided to put this desire into action on a specific case. The case was that of the most notorious criminal in the news at the moment, Henri Pranzini, who had been sentenced to death by guillotine for the murder, in the course of a robbery in Paris, of a rich lady, her child and her maid. He was abused and reviled in the press, adding to his infamy by maintaining his innocence and showing no sign of compunction or repentance. 'I could do nothing myself,' Thérèse says, 'but I could offer to God our Lord's infinite merits.' She asked Céline to get a Mass said for Pranzini, and admits that she was too shy to make such a request herself. Céline

68

joined in the campaign of prayer. With the audacity of innocence, Thérèse asked God to give her some sign that their
prayers had been answered – although, of course, even without
any sign, she would still believe that God had pardoned the poor
man. On the day after the execution, she read in her father's copy
of *La Croix* how, just as Pranzini 'was preparing to put his head
between the bars of the guillotine, he turned to the priest who
was holding out the crucifix to him and kissed, three times, the
sacred wounds. And with that, his soul went to receive its reward.' She mentions, in passing, that although 'Papa didn't
allow us to read newspapers, I thought there could be no harm
in following up the story of Pranzini.' Obviously, Thérèse was
taking a more comprehensive view of things now from that of
the girl who, not long before, had been tormented by scruples
about the morality of every thought and action in her life.

While continuing her studies in history and science, Thérèse
concentrated even more on her spiritual reading. Like many
souls before and since, her favourite book was *The Imitation of
Christ* by the Augustinian monk, Thomas à Kempis (1380-1471).
'For a long time past,' she writes of this period, 'what kept me
going was the wholemeal bread you get in *The Imitation of Christ*.
I found nothing else really useful, until I began to discover the
treasures hidden in the gospels. Dear *Imitation*! I knew nearly all
the chapters by heart, but nothing would part me from my little
book; it lived in my pocket during the summer, and in my muff
during the winter … it was a favourite joke at my aunt's to open
it at random and "put me on" at whichever chapter she came to.'

Anyone who has had the good fortune to read and benefit
from the book will appreciate the achievement of a fourteen-
year-old girl in having memorised *The Imitation of Christ* (she
must have been introduced to it at an early age; it probably
formed part of those evening spiritual readings which were part
of the domestic scene). Readers who have not come across it
might be encouraged to open their minds and souls to this trea-
sury of wisdom and spirituality by considering the following,
which is the opening paragraph of the Introduction to a modern

translation by Leo Sherley-Price (Penguin Classics, 1952): 'It would be impossible to estimate the wide and profound influence that this wonderful little book has exercised throughout Christendom for over five hundred years. After the Bible itself, no other work can compare with its profound wisdom, clarity of thought, and converting power. Christians of such widely differing period and outlook as St Thomas More and General Gordon, St Ignatius Loyola and John Wesley, St Francis Xavier and Dr Johnson, are but a few of the thousands who have acknowledged their debt to this golden work.'

The popularity and influence of the *Imitation* can also be seen in literature. In his great novel, *War and Peace*, Tolstoy has his main character, the philosophical Pierre, 'spending whole days reading Thomas à Kempis' in his quest for a meaning to life – the fact that Tolstoy does not name the book itself would indicate that it must have been well known in Russia. George Eliot puts quotations from the *Imitation* in the mouths of characters in her novel, *The Mill on the Floss*, and – surely the most quaint of all references, but not, of course, to those who are familiar with the idiosyncratic brilliance of Elia – in his essay, *My Relations*, Charles Lamb (1775-1834) says: 'I had an aunt, a dear and good one. She was one whom single blessedness had soured to the world. She often used to say, I was the only thing in it which she loved; and, when she thought I was quitting it, she grieved over me with a mother's tears ... She was from morning till night poring over good books and devotional exercises. Her favourite volumes were Thomas à Kempis, in Stanhope's translation; and a Roman Catholic Prayer Book, with the matins and complines regularly set down – terms which I was at that time too young to understand. She persisted in reading them, although admonished daily concerning their Papistical tendency; and went to church every Sabbath, as a good Protestant should do.' One can infer that Elia himself was a fan and a beneficiary of the *Imitation* – perhaps that eccentric aunt bequeathed him her own well-read copy.

In Book One of the *Imitation* there is a chapter on Judgement and the Punishment of Sinners which, in its traditional medieval imagery of the fires of hell, is more in tune with the kind of fiery sermons preached at Thérèse and the other First Communicants by the stern Fr Domin than with the loving spirituality developing in her soul since her release from the mental maze of her scruples. Medieval artists tried to portray the torments of the damned in visual terms for an illiterate public, and even the great Dante, in the *Inferno* cantos of the *Divina Commedia*, paints similar graphic pictures in verse of those tit-for-tat torments with which preachers and writers like the author of the *Imitation* sought to frighten sinners into repentance. 'In whatever things a man sins,' says Thomas à Kempis, 'in those will he be the more severely punished. Then will the slothful be spurred by fiery goads, and the gluttonous tormented by dire hunger and thirst. Then will the luxurious and pleasure-loving be plunged into burning pitch and stinking sulphur, while the envious will howl their grief like wild dogs.' And so on, and so on!

To the modern reader, if such catalogues of eternal physical torture are wrenched from the context of their historical time, they will seem to depict God in the role of a vengeful and calculating deity who delights in matching each vice with its appropriate retribution, not unlike Gilbert and Sullivan's eponymous *Mikado* who sings: 'My object all sublime, I shall achieve in time – to let the punishment fit the crime, the punishment fit the crime.' It should be noted, however, that before the end of that same brief chapter, Thomas says: 'All, therefore, is vanity, save to love God and serve him alone. For he who loves God fears neither death, punishment, judgement, nor hell; for perfect love enjoys sure access to God.' Chapter 15 of Book I is entitled, *On deeds done out of love,* and there the young Thérèse would have read: 'Without love, the outward work is of no value; but whatever is done out of love, be it never so little, is wholly fruitful. For God regards the greatness of the love that prompts an action, rather than the greatness of the deed itself.' That is almost a blueprint for the 'little way' of love and trust by which Thérèse was to achieve sainthood.

Having thus acknowledged her debt to the 'wholemeal bread' of *The Imitation of Christ*, Sister Thérèse, looking back at herself in her new and self-assured persona, says: 'But I was fourteen now, and developing a taste for wider reading.' This, by contrast, she calls the 'oil and honey' more suitable to her more mature development., and the book in which this came to her was impressively entitled, *Fin du Monde Presente et Mystères de la Vie Future (The End of the Present World and the Mysteries of the Future Life)*. Both the book and its author, the Abbé Arminjon, like many such, are forgotten; but if it affected other souls as it did the soul of the future saint, it must indeed have been a source of the spiritual 'oil and honey' Thérèse tasted in it. Its effect on her she sums up thus: 'All the tremendous truths of religion, all the mysteries of eternity, came flooding into my soul with a feeling of happiness that had nothing to do with this world.'

This book was probably read also by Céline who was now, says Thérèse, 'the privileged confidante of my thoughts – the difference in age didn't matter, because I'd grown so much in size and still more because I'd grown so much in grace.' They took to having, at the window in the upper room with a view, conversations on spiritual matters, the memory of which inspires Sister Thérèse to quote the mystical Carmelite poet, St John of the Cross, and to compare those earnest chats between the two teenage sisters to the conversations between St Monica and St Augustine, also at a window with a view, at 'Ostia upon the Tiber,' as Augustine recalls in his great spiritual autobiography, the *Confessions*, 'where we were preparing to pass over the sea into Africa'. Monica never completed that homeward journey, but died at Ostia some days later.

Enclosed within the walls of her convent, the poet in Sister Thérèse is moved to a lyrical passage as she recalls those quiet evening conversations with her sister: 'Our eyes were lost in distance as we watched the pale moon rising slowly above the height of the trees. Those silvery rays she cast on a sleeping world, the stars shining bright in the blue vault above us, the fleecy clouds floating by in the evening wind – how everything conspired to turn our thoughts towards heaven!'

The spiritual 'honey and oil' she absorbed from that book by Abbé Arminjon obviously had a profound effect on Thérèse, but the interesting thing about this book for us is that it was loaned to Louis Martin by the Carmelite nuns, and it was with his permission that his youngest daughter read it. This indicates that he was in regular and friendly contact with the community where he now had two daughters. It also causes the reader to surmise that those eldest daughters must have discussed with their father, during his visits, the situation and future of the youngest of his five daughters, Thérèse, whose vocation to Carmel had been a matter of family awareness for years already. It cannot have been a great surprise to him to hear it finally from Thérèse herself, certainly not a shock like the one he experienced on that day in Alençon when the middle daughter, Léonie, had gone to visit the Poor Clares and stayed with them (Léonie was currently in her second attempt at the religious life, having entered the Order of the Visitation at Caen; this time she stayed for nearly six months, until ill-health forced her home again, in time to see Thérèse enter Carmel).

Sister Thérèse, recording it in her manuscript, makes a very moving and dramatic scene of the occasion, on the afternoon of Pentecost Sunday, in May 1887, when she went to her father in the garden at *Les Buissonets* and told him formally that she wished to enter Carmel. She was aware of his frail state of health – he had recently suffered the first slight stroke, causing some hours of partial paralysis, in a series that was to reduce him eventually to a physical and mental wreck of the fine man Thérèse adored. 'How was I to tell Papa?' she writes. 'He had already given his three eldest daughters to religion; how to break it to him that he must say goodbye to his favourite?' She had chosen Pentecost as the most suitable day, and prayed to the apostles: 'After all, it was up to them to help me overcome my timidity: the Carmelite vocation which God had marked out for me meant evangelising by prayer and acts of sacrifice, the church's evangelists.'

Louis saw her coming, and if he read her mind, he still played his part lovingly. 'I went up and sat there beside him,' she writes, 'without saying a single word, but my eyes were wet with tears. He looked down at me ever so tenderly, and pressed my head close to his heart: "What's the matter, little princess?" he said. "Tell me about it." Then he got up, as if to disguise his own feelings, and began to walk up and down, still holding me close to his side.' Before agreeing to her request, he made only the tentative and obvious objection that she was very young; then, having listened to her earnest arguments, he said: 'What an honour God is doing me, in asking me like this for the gift of one daughter after another!' Remembering, surely, the day when, high in the Swiss Alps, the twenty-year-old Louis Martin picked a little white flower which he brought home as a souvenir and treasured for years, the sixty-four-year old Louis now turned to where some similar little white flowers were growing on a low wall. He picked one and gave it to Thérèse, pointing out how God had cared for it and kept it in being. The little flower was to become the symbol of her life, and even the affectionate name by which she would be known to the faithful of the Catholic Church. 'I put the flower between the leaves of my *Imitation*,' Sister Thérèse writes, 'marking the chapter on the duty of loving God above all things.' She had recorded that her father plucked the little flower complete with its roots, and this indicated that it was destined to take root in a new and more fruitful soil, that of Carmel, than the soft moss of a garden wall at *Les Buissonets*. Now, however, the ailing Sister Thérèse writes with a resigned foreboding: 'There it remains (in her copy of the *Imitation*), only the stalk had broken off now, close to the roots, as if God meant to tell me that he's going to sever my connection with this earth before long, instead of leaving me to fade away gradually.'

Her beloved father having consented, albeit tearfully, and already encouraged both by her sister, Pauline, now five years in Carmel, and the Prioress, Mother Gonzague – they must both have agreed on the suspension, in the case of their unique young applicant, of the Carmelite rules which forbade, respectively, the admission to the same community of more than two members of the same family, and the acceptance in any convent of an applicant under twenty-one years of age – Thérèse, with her new-found confidence, saw no obstacle in her way to admission to Carmel, and actually decided on an appropriate time for that event, either at Christmas or on the date of her birthday, 2 January 1888, when she would be all of fifteen years old. She was to discover that the road to Carmel was not the smooth pathway she imagined, but a road strewn with obstacles that would severely test whether her wish to enter at so young an age was a genuine call from the Holy Spirit or a girlish fancy to follow her older sisters into what she might have imagined as a protected environment of piety and peace.

Her first pyschological setback must have occurred when she found that her eldest sister, Marie, did not agree with her spiritual 'mother', Pauline, in approving her entry. Marie had not yet been a year in Carmel, and she probably felt that the change from the luxury of the Martin home to the rigours of the Carmel life would be too much for their youngest sister who had been petted and coddled from childhood. A more serious obstacle was the refusal of Isidore Guérin, Thérèse's maternal uncle, to give his consent, which was apparently essential in the circumstances. 'He couldn't have been kinder,' Sister Thérèse writes – knowing, as she has obviously been advised by her sister and Prioress, Mother Agnes, that the said Uncle is likely to see this manuscript some time – 'but he flatly refused to give his permission – I wasn't to raise the subject of my vocation with him till I had turned seventeen. It would be the height of imprudence, he said, to admit a child of fifteen to the life of Carmel, which, by general consent, was a life of mature reflection, whereas I had no experience of the world. What would people say?' Some commentators suggest that what people would say is exactly what was troubling Uncle Isidore Guérin. As a professional man, and in his social life, he did not relish the gossip that might ensue if, the three eldest girls of his widowed brother-in-law, Louis Martin, having already abandoned their comfortable home and their prospects of a suitable marriage to lock themselves away in religious orders, they were now to be followed by a fifteen-year-old whom Isidore had long considered to be weakly sentimental and childish.

Uncle Isidore resorted to the religious language he knew Thérèse would appreciate: nothing short of a miracle, he said, would make him change his mind. Whereupon, inevitably, Thérèse began to pray for just that! Just as inevitably, three days later, Uncle Isidore had changed his mind. When Thérèse called to see him again, he was a different man, all sweetness and light. Thérese did not know that, in the meantime, Pauline had written to Uncle Isidore. It will be seen also that, more than likely, Louis had responded to his daughter's disappointment by going to have a chat with his brother-in-law. Isidore first gently told Thérèse that she need not be afraid of him – who told him that she always had been inhibited by his attitude to her? – and then that she need not go on praying for a miracle, because it had already happened. 'He had asked God to make up his mind for him,' she writes, 'and his prayer had been answered.' And now, for the objective reader, the significant part of her account: 'He said I was a flower God had decided to pick while it was still in the bud, and he wasn't going to stand in the way.' One can hear a distinct echo of the voice of her father in the garden scene at *Les Buissonets* some days earlier.

A few days later, when Thérèse went with her father and Céline for their regular visit to Carmel, she was eager to tell Pauline and Marie the glad news of Uncle Isidore's consent to her entry; she was forestalled by their bad news – the elderly priest, Fr Delatroëtte, who was the ecclesiastical superior of the convent and as such had to approve the entry of any applicant, resolutely refused to allow Thérèse to enter until she reached the appointed age of twenty-one. Thérèse, accompanied by her father, went to see the priest, but his answer to her arguments and her father's supporting approval was that he was abiding by the rules, and that only the bishop could cause him to change his ruling. To the bishop, therefore, they resolved to go.

While waiting for an appointment to visit Bishop Hugonin at Bayeux, Thérèse joined her sister, Céline, in putting religious faith into charitable practice: they cared in their own house for two little girls, the daughters of a poor woman who was dying (she was a relative of the family maid) and whose five children would be left orphans. It caused Thérèse, herself the youngest and spoilt child of five in a wealthy family, to learn something of the harsher lot dealt out to other children, although she can hardly have appreciated that those unfortunate urchins were more likely to remember longer the good food and comfort of that short spell in *Les Buissonets* than the spiritual lessons she zealously gave them about heaven and the Child Jesus.

For her interview with Bishop Hugonin in October 1887, perhaps on advice from her sisters in Carmel, Thérèse decided to make herself look older by 'putting up her hair'. An extant photograph, taken a few months later, shows the 'crowning glory' above the bright-eyed intelligent face of a smiling and confident young lady. But while both the bishop and his vicar-general, M. Révérony, who was present, were charmed by her personality and her earnestness, the only result of the interview was that the new coiffure became a topic for gentle joking by the elderly bishop when Thérèse's father unwisely told him of her ploy. 'This wasn't forgotten,' Sister Thérèse recalls ruefully, 'the bishop never talked about "that little daughter of mine" without telling the story about my hair.' The bishop, like the priest at the convent, thought Thérèse too young for the rigours of life in an enclosed order; he also suggested that she would be a comfort to her father if she stayed at home for some years more, and was surprised when the same father intervened to say that he had no objection to Thérèse's entry. When poor Thérèse defeated the purpose of her new hair-style by breaking down in tears, the bishop comforted her kindly. He also told her that he would be visiting Lisieux the following week and would have a talk about her with the Curé of Saint-Jacques, the priest who had objected to her entry.

When Louis told him that he had already arranged to take

Thérèse and her older sister, Céline, on a pilgrimage to Rome, and that Thérèse, should this present application fail, intended to petition the Holy Father himself, the bishop encouraged her, while privately he may have been thinking that Pope Leo XIII had enough local and universal problems to deal with not to pay much attention to the personal problem of this young girl from France – after the loss of the papal states and the completion of Italian unity with the fall of Rome in 1870, followed by the refusal of Leo's successor, Pope Pius IX, to compromise with the anti-clerical parliament and, in protest, his decision to confine himself to the limits of the Vatican and its gardens, the Pope would be known as 'the Prisoner of the Vatican' until Mussolini signed his tactical political concordat with the papacy in 1929.

CHAPTER TEN

Meeting the Pope

Only three days after the interview with Bishop Hugonin, Louis Martin and his two daughters set off for Paris from where the pilgrimage to Rome was to begin early in November. 'Papa took us to Paris a few days early,' Thérèse says, 'to see the sights.' Not a very devotional start to a pilgrimage, one might consider; in reality, the pilgrimage was more a month-long tour of Italy, with a week in Rome and an audience with the Pope as the central feature. 'The pilgrims mostly belonged to the world of high society,' Thérèse writes, 'which was quite a new experience for Céline and me; but we weren't dazzled by it at all – these titles and handles to people's names, we felt, were so much smoke'; and she backs up her disdain with a quote from the wise author of *The Imitation of Christ*. From other sources we learn that the pilgrimage was to honour the fiftieth anniversary of the ordination to the priesthood of Pope Leo XIII, and that the group of about two hundred included over seventy priests and thirty titled people.

Thérèse does not advert to the expense involved in the month-long tour, but she does record one of the incidental insights she picked up: 'Another discovery I made was about priests.' She had been puzzled, she says, about the statement in the Carmelite Rule that the chief object of the order was to pray for sinners and priests. 'Pray for sinners, by all means, but why priests?' Although she maintains that the priests she met were 'good, holy priests,' she formed the opinion that 'priests have their frailties and their weaknesses, like other men.' She should have been prepared for this learning process by her reading of *The Imitation of Christ* where a chapter in Book Four is devoted to

'The dignity of the priestly office.' And if she had known the philosophical treatise, *Utopia*, by the martyred English statesman, Thomas More, she would have read how, in his ideal state, there would be 'few priests – but good ones'. However, Sister Thérèse appreciates now the object of all the prayers and sacrifices the enclosed nuns make: 'We have to pray for the priests while they are busy bringing souls to Christ by their preaching – and still more by their example.' She concludes enigmatically: 'But I mustn't go on about that: I should never stop.'

In Paris, Thérèse was able to visit the church of Notre Dame des Victoires and to thank Our Lady once again for her intercession in the cure that had put a sudden end to the mysterious and debilitating illness of her schooldays – it was at that same church that Louis had arranged a novena of Masses for her recovery. Remembering how she had suffered later from scruples concerning the circumstances of that cure, she writes: 'Our Lady gave me the assurance that she really had smiled at me, really had effected my cure. I knew then that she really was watching over me, that I was her child – I began calling her Mamma because Mother didn't seem intimate enough.' (Was she still subconsciously suffering from the loss of her natural mother and of those other 'mothers' with whom she had tried to replace her?) She also prayed to Our Lady and St Joseph to protect her from any evil she might encounter on the journey.

As she sets out to give an account of the great experience, Sister Thérèse strikes an apologetic note from which we learn the difficult circumstances in which this already ailing young nun was trying to fulfil the task imposed on her by religious obedience (she would soon be coughing up blood and would be dead within a little over two years): 'And now, dear Mother, I'm going to tell you traveller's tales; too many of them, maybe, and I'm not sure but that they may bore you – I can't properly plan beforehand what I'm going to write, because it all has to be done at odd moments in my free time.' And we shall see later how the well-meant but bothersome interruptions by other nuns made her task all the more wearisome.

Of that month-long journey, by train from city to city, by horse-carriage sight-seeing in each city, 'Rome was our goal,' Thérèse says, 'but there were plenty of wonderful experiences on the way there.' Her account suggests that she kept a diary of the journey. While she enjoyed the natural beauty of Switzerland, as her father, now her guide, had done in his youth, the main objects of her interest in each city they visited – Milan, Venice, Padua, Bologna, Loreto, Rome itself – were the churches and the relics. She seems not to have questioned then, or to doubt now, the validity of any of the latter: 'At Holy Cross church in Rome,' she recalls, 'we venerated several relics of the true Cross, as well as two of the Thorns and one of the Nails, all enclosed in a magnificent gold reliquary with no glass in it. So when my turn came I managed to put my little finger through one of the holes, and actually touched one of the Nails which had been bathed in the precious Blood.'

At Loreto, they visited the house reputed to have been transported miraculously from Nazareth – 'The basilica is only a marble casket in which the Holy House reposes like a precious diamond.' The innocent piety of the young Thérèse survives in the ecstatic account penned by the mature Sister Thérèse of the Child Jesus: 'I can't tell you how deeply I was moved to share the same roof, as it were, with the Holy Family. On these walls our divine Redeemer had gazed; on this ground the sweat had fallen from Joseph's brow; here Mary had carried, in and out, the Child of her virginal womb. To have seen the little room in which the angel greeted her, to have put my rosary-beads for a moment in the bowl from which the Child Jesus had eaten – those are things you can't remember without a thrill.' That they were not remembered with more critical scrutiny will puzzle the modern reader.

Her opinion of the city that was in that same period enchanting writers like Henry James and Thomas Mann, indicates a capacity for such criticism: 'Venice, for all its charm,' she comments, 'struck me as a melancholy place.' Bologna made an even worse impression; this had nothing to do with its churches or

relics, but with the typically Italian notice taken of those two attractive young French girls by the university students 'who
crowded its streets and hedged us in whenever we went about
on foot'. Even as the train arrived in Bologna, one of those jovial
students earned himself a special black mark in her diary – he
gallantly lifted her down from the train to the platform, much to
her annoyance both as a self-assured teenager and a prospective
future Carmelite.

As has been seen from her comments about priests, Thérèse
was also observing the behaviour of those around her. 'One saw
so many different sides of human character,' she recalls, and
comments, 'what a fascinating study the world is, when you are
just going to say goodbye to it.' She noted the misanthropic reaction to everything – hotels, towns, people, carriages – of one
cranky old man among the pilgrims and the charitable efforts of
her father to cheer him up. On a more personal note, she
shrewdly spotted that the Vicar-General, M Révérony, who had
been present at her interview with the bishop, was keeping an
eye on her behaviour. 'I'd see him looking at me from a distance,
and when I wasn't facing him at table he'd manage to lean forward and get a good look at me, or listen to what I said. His cur-
iosity was natural; he wanted to know if I really was fit for the
Carmelite life.' Obviously, the kind old Bishop Huganin, who
was not on the pilgrimage, also wanted to know, and the report
he got must have been positive.

There were six days of sight-seeing in Rome before the audience with the Pope. Expecting to kneel and kiss the holy ground
of the Colosseum, 'the arena in which so many martyrs had shed
their blood for Christ', Thérèse was disappointed to find the
arena 'no better than a mass of fallen masonry, which the unfortunate pilgrim has to contemplate from behind a barrier.' This
did not deter herself and Céline. Waiting till their group had
passed on with the guide, they clambered over the railings, ig-
nored their astonished father's order to come back, and made
their way down the piles of rubble. They kissed a spot Céline
had heard the informative guide point out 'as the place where

the martyrs actually suffered', collected a few small stones, and climbed back up. Louis did not know whether to scold them or admire their audacity and agility. The Catacombs offered another opportunity for their innocent mixture of piety with devotional vandalism; again waiting for the group to move on, they scraped some earth from the area around the burial site of St Cecilia.

The visit to the Church of St Agnes had a special significance – Sister Agnes of Jesus was the name in religion of their sister, Pauline. Thérèse would have liked to bring back some special souvenir from this church to Pauline, her 'second mother'. Fortunately for the guardians of that church and its treasures, 'the only one I managed to get was a little red stone which had somehow come loose from a rich mosaic – dating back to the time of St Agnes, so that her eyes must often have rested on it.' Her comment is interesting, in that it was not written on the day by the enthusiastic teenage pilgrim, but years later by the twenty-two-year old nun: 'Dear saint, how charming of her to make me a present of the exact thing we were looking for, a relic, when it was against all the rules that we should have one!' Sister Thérèse of the Child Jesus, aspiring through her 'little way' of love, prayer and suffering, to become a saint, seems to be wryly admitting that Thérèse Martin, the fourteen-year-old enthusiastic pilgrim, had a long way to go on the road to sanctity.

While such actions and comments might indicate some lingering immaturity, other observations, some already noted, show the development in Thérèse of adult judgement and evaluation of life and society. One passage in this section will come as a surprise to the modern reader and perhaps cause some agnostic feminists to review their evaluation of nuns and saints: 'I still can't understand why it's so easy for a woman to get excommunicated in Italy! All the time, people seemed to be saying: "No, you mustn't go here, you mustn't go there; you'll be excommunicated." There's no respect for us poor wretched women anywhere. And yet you'll find the love of God much commoner among women than among men, and the women at the

Crucifixion showed much more courage than the apostles, exposing themselves to insult, and wiping Our Lord's face. I suppose he lets us share the neglect he himself chose for his lot on earth; in heaven, where the last shall be first, we shall know more about what God thinks.' One wonders what the Pope, cardinals and bishops thought when they read that broadside from an enclosed young nun when *Histoire d'une âme* became a best-seller after her death.

Finally, the occasion that was for Thérèse the whole focus of the pilgrimage arrived. 'On Sunday, the 20th of November, we put on our ceremonial dress – black, with a lace mantilla, and a large Papal medal on a ribbon of blue and white – and made our way through the Vatican to the Pope's own chapel.' Thus Thérèse begins her account of her audience with Pope Leo XIII, an event that could make a dramatic scene in a play or film about her life but that was to end for her in disappointment and tears. Having assisted at the Mass celebrated by the 77-year-old Pontiff at 8 am, and a Mass of thanksgiving that followed, the pilgrims were admitted to the audience chamber where the Pope sat in a big armchair, surrounded by cardinals and archbishops, papal guards and officials. The French contingent were to be introduced by M Révérony, Vicar-Apostolic, who instructed them in the protocol – each person would kneel before the Pope, kiss his foot and his hand, receive his blessing, and depart, without speaking. That order, coming from such a source, dismayed Thérèse, but she was encouraged by Céline to make use of this one chance in a lifetime.

When her turn came, she did just that. The Pope, who was not in good health, and who was probably just going through the usual motions of an audience, was startled out of his routine blessing when the young girl kneeling before him suddenly spoke, and in French.

'Most Holy Father,' she said, 'I have a great favour to ask of you.' As his dark eyes fixed on her, she went on, 'In honour of your jubilee, I want you to let me enter the Carmelite order at fifteen.' No wonder the poor man turned his puzzled face to the

French Vicar-General and said: 'I don't understand.' M Révérony, just as surprised as the Pope but knowing what it was all about, quickly and probably with a grimace at the disobedient girl who had defied the protocol, explained, 'Most Holy Father, this child here is anxious to enter Carmel at fifteen – and her superiors are looking into the matter at this moment.' That addendum provided a helpful hint for the Pope and a damper on the plea of Thérèse. The Pope looked at the young girl with kindness and said gently, 'Very well, my child, do what your superiors tell you.' He must have felt a tinge of irritation when the girl kneeling before him put her hands on his knees and spoke even more urgently: 'Yes, Most Holy Father, but if you would say the word, everybody would agree.' The trusting compliment was lost on the tired Pope; but he still spoke kindly and with paternal emphasis: 'Go now, all is well, if God wants you to enter, you will.' At which point, probably in response to an indication from the exasperated Vicar-General, two Papal guards took Thérèse by the arms and, with the assistance of the VG himself, carried her bodily away to the exit door where another guard presented the tearful girl with the routine gift of a papal medal, little consolation for what seemed to be the final setback to her hopes. When the men of the party came up in their turn, M Révérony made some amends for his rough handling of Thérèse by introducing her father to the Pope: 'Here is the father of two Carmelite nuns,' he said, and the Pope placed his hand on the head of Louis Martin as in a special blessing.

Thérèse might have considered her appeal to the Pope a failure, but her devout father, impressed by her courage and determination, tried a new resource on her behalf. He was acquainted with an elderly French religious in Rome named Br Siméon, a member of the Brothers of the Christian Schools, who was highly regarded in Vatican circles, being the founder and director of the leading Catholic secondary school for boys in Rome, a school attended by relatives of many Vatican dignitaries and officials, including the grandnephews of the Pope himself. Louis and his brother-in-law, Isidore Guérin, were both associated with the

Christian Schools in Lisieux and Alençon. In renewing his acquaintence with Br Siméon, Louis took the opportunity to discuss the vocation of Thérèse and her desire, even at so young an age, to follow her sisters into Carmel. Br Siméon was so impressed that he took notes of what Louis told him. A further positive note was added when the Vicar-General, M Révérony, also a friend of Br Siméon, called in while they were speaking together and assured Louis that, although he had no alternative but to behave as he did at the papal audience, he was sincerely impressed with Thérèse's character and sincerity, and would do all in his power to help her.

He must have kept his word, as will be seen. When, after another ten days of sightseeing that took in Naples, Pompeii, Assisi, Florence, Pisa, Genoa, Marseilles and Lyons, Louis and his two daughters finally reached home, Thérèse could hardly wait to visit Pauline in the convent and let her know what had happened when she made her plea, not now to the Vicar Apostolic of the diocese, but to the Vicar of Christ on earth. Pauline advised her to write to the bishop and remind him of his promise to consider her request – Thérèse still hoped against hope that she would be able to enter Carmel at Christmas. Uncle Isidore, ever the vigilant critic, was not satisfied with Thérèse's letter and re-wrote it; then Pauline wrote to tell her not to post it just yet (something must have been going on behind the scenes). It was finally posted ten days before Christmas. Meanwhile, Bishop Hugonin had had plenty of time to listen to the report of his Vicar-General, M Révérony. On 28 December, he wrote to Mother Gonzague, Prioress of the Carmelite convent, and told her that he would leave the decision up to her, thus overruling the firmly negative decision of Fr Delatroëtte, the ecclesiastical superior of the convent.

Mother Gonzague had been charmed by Thérèse from her first meeting with her when the young girl came with her family to visit Pauline, the first of the Martin girls to enter Carmel. She was therefore surprised when it was Pauline who now proposed that Thérèse should not be admitted just then. Pauline's concern was that the approaching season of Lent, with its increased pentitential exercises and fasting, might prove too severe an introduction to the life of Carmel for her fifteen-year-old sister. Thérèse, disappointed at first, came to accept the wisdom of Pauline's decision. She decided to spend the intervening three months in a personal retreat of prayer and preparation. She wrote to the Vicar General and to Fr Delatroëtte to thank them; from the first she received a gracious reply, from the latter, a response less enthusiastic. He promised 'to pray with my whole heart that you will be worthy of being a Carmelite,' and then added caustically, 'I cannot refrain from regretting that you pressed for your entrance with so much insistence. I fear that later on you and your own sisters will have to regret it.'

On 6 January, Léonie came home from the Visitation Convent at Caen, her ill health putting an end to her second attempt at entering the religious life. Three months later, on 2 April, Thérèse entered Carmel. The night before, the family and relatives gathered for a farewell dinner. 'And so,' Thérèse writes, 'on the morning of the great day itself, I took a last look at *Les Buissonets*, the beloved cradle of my childhood's years, which I was never to see again. And then, with dear Papa giving me his arm, I set out to climb the hillside of Carmel.'

CHAPTER ELEVEN

A Little Flower Transplanted

If Sister Thérèse had kept strictly to the directions given her when her sister, Pauline, ordered her, as Prioress, to write down her memories of her childhood, the manuscript should have ended with her entry into Carmel, an event which was definitely the end of what had been a prolonged childhood. However, as has been noticed already, even if the manuscript had ended at that point, it would not have been merely a chronicle of the first fifteen years in the life of the author.

As she took up her pen, albeit reluctantly, to comply with the order of her Prioress and sister, Sister Thérèse of the Child Jesus was a very different person from the eager but somewhat naïve teenager, Thérèse Martin, who 'climbed the hillside of Carmel' leaning on the arm of her beloved Papa nearly seven years earlier. She was now a nun who was mystical in her spirituality but who also, paradoxically, had long been suffering deprivation of the solace found in prayer and devotional practices by common souls. She was also unwell – she had only two and a half years more of life left to her – and her recording of the events of her childhood was inevitably influenced by her religious upbringing and by her present forebodings regarding death and eternity. Inevitably, then, her narrative often digresses into discursive passages and sections of spiritually meditative comment that have their origin in the soul of the nun rather than in her factual and sentimental recollections of childhood days.

The memoir she finally handed to Mother Agnes a year later, on 20 January 1896, actually extends into an account of her life in Carmel up to that time. On the final page, she says: 'There, Mother, that's all I can tell you about the life of your youngest sister. You yourself know far better than I do what I am, and what our Lord has done for me; so, you won't mind my having compressed my life as a religious within such narrow limits.' Thérèse herself was obviously aware that she had gone far beyond the story of her childhood. This could have been as a result of further discussion between herself and Mother Agnes, although there is no record of such a development. She seems also to have thought she was finished with writing, as well as having a premonition of her early death. 'How is it going to end,' she asks herself, 'this story which I've called the story of a little white flower? Perhaps it will be picked, still fresh …'

In describing the events of her years in Carmel, Thérèse continues as she has done with regard to the story of her childhood. She records her own progress through the stages of profession, as well as events like the catastrophic influenza epidemic of 1891 which killed over 70,000 people in Europe – a foretaste of the slaughter wrought by another and greater flu epidemic subsequent to the slaughter in the trenches during the 1914-18 war. When the outbreak of 1891 arrived in the Carmel of Lisieux, it claimed three victims in the small community. The nineteen-year-old Sister Thérèse, along with her eldest sister, Marie, and one other nun, being the only ones unaffected, had to tend to the sick and dying. She is telling these things to her sister, Pauline, Mother Agnes, who at this stage has been Prioress for the past two years, and who, like the majority of the nuns, knows about them already. It was therefore the complementary aspect of her narrative, her analysis of spiritual trials and the social sufferings consequent on 'the little white flower' having been transplanted from the comfort of *Les Buissonets* to the disciplined life in Carmel, that really alerted Mother Agnes and others to the unique value of what Sister Thérèse had written.

Through all of this section of *The Story of a Soul*, and similarly through the other autobiographical manuscript, the one written for Mother Marie de Gonzague, the modern reader will need to make allowance for the milieu in which they were written. We are all conditioned by the circumstances of the age in which we live, and the multi-media influence on our present society and civilisation of the technological developments of the twentieth century is a matter for future social historians to assess. A reader whose experience has been mainly in the area of pulp fiction, whether of the erotic novelette or the action thriller, and who suddenly decides to read Herman Melville's *Moby Dick*, published in 1851 and considered by many critics to be the greatest novel in the English language, will not get very far in that unique literary and philosophical experience unless intelligence and resolve prevail over habit and indifference. Similarly, anyone who comes to *The Story of a Soul* with a mind whose critical faculties have been conditioned by the trivia and banalities, the sensationalism, scandalmongering and pornography of our mass media, will need to insert a blank disk in the mental computer (a concept with which children of our era are familiar but which would mean nothing to the intellectuals of former times).

Sister Thérèse Martin could only pen her story 'at odd moments', as she said herself, and by the light of a faulty little oil-lamp, in an unheated cell in that small convent in France in the final decade of the nineteenth century. She produced her manuscripts on odd pages or in notebooks at the behest of religious superiors, one of them her own eldest sister, who, initially at least, were meant to be her only readers. No modern reader should be surprised to find that her life-story is not told in the style of some modern celebrity or showbiz personality commissioned by a commercial publisher to supply a sensational autobiography (often through the talented medium of a ghost-writer, credited or not).

Writing of the harsh treatment she received from Mother Gonzague in her early days in Carmel, Thérèse says: 'I hardly ever met her without having to kiss the ground for something I'd done wrong' (perhaps, on those occasions, her mind went back to the day when the child Thérèse stubbornly rejected her mother's testing offer of a financial reward if she would kiss the floor?). In some of the more personal passages in her autobiography, where she is directly addressing either Mother Gonzague or Mother Agnes, or when referring to relatives and others, Sister Thérèse uses language that seems cloying or even flattering. It was the style of the period, a form of social and religious etiquette, just as the humiliating act of kissing the ground for faults, real or contrived, was part of the accepted method of training in the religious life. But we have already seen that Sister Thérèse was quite capable of sharp and percipient comment on people and affairs, and was far ahead of her time in some of the opinions she expressed on religious and social matters.

When she writes on the spiritual developments in her own soul, she herself recognises the difficulty of describing her ecstatic mystical experiences and the converse interior anguish of her spiritual trials and tribulations. In the introductory pages of the brief personal manuscript, addressing her sister and godmother, Marie (Sister Marie of the Sacred Heart) who had asked her to write an account of her spiritual experiences during a recent retreat, she says: 'How am I to express heavenly mysteries in the language of earth?' And in the final pages of the third manuscript, shortly before the pencil was finally to drop from her fingers, she says, '… what I've tried to write about is a bit difficult to follow.' In many places, she resorts to speaking directly to God or to the Child Jesus who was her patron, and here again it will take the modern reader by surprise to find the familiar, even sentimental, language she uses, as well as her spiritual use of the symbolic concepts, largely adapted from the Bible's Song of Songs, of the lover, of marriage, and even of maternity. In Book One of Thérèse's beloved *Imitation of Christ* there is a brief chapter entitled, *On the Reading of Holy Scriptures*, in which we are given the fundamental counsel: 'All sacred scriptures should be read in the spirit in which they were written.' In that same spirit we should humbly submit our own souls to the experience of reading *The Story of a Soul*. For those who would like to go further, there are many commentaries and studies available.

Let us now return to the fifteen-year-old Thérèse as she crosses the threshold of Carmel where she will live, hidden from the outside world, until her death over nine years later.

On that day when she entered Carmel, young Mlle Martin was probably, as regards the religious life, the best-informed postulant ever to arrive there. She had been a regular visitor to the convent where her two older sisters were already members of the community, Pauline for six years, Marie for two. In conversation and in letters, they had prepared her for the change from the comfort of a wealthy home life to the more rudimentary conditions of life in what one of them described as a poor convent. 'I had no illusions at all, thank God, when I entered Carmel,' she writes. 'I found the religious life exactly what I had expected it to be.' In the light of some of her subsequent comments, that statement will appear to be ambiguous and open to interpretation.

Thérèse was also well known to the other nuns, having been a constant visitor since the day Pauline entered. The nuns had thus seen her grow from a pretty child of nine to the confident young teenager who now arrived, having had the rules regarding entry set aside on her behalf by authority of the bishop himself, as the latest addition to their small community. Their subsequent behaviour towards Thérèse, including that of the Prioress, Mother Gonzague, indicates their awareness of two factors that would not have applied to any other postulant. Firstly, they had to substitute an impersonal and detached attitude for the fond and almost maternal concern they had felt for Thérèse from the day when she first appeared as the youngest daughter of the respected Monsieur Martin and the motherless sister of their new postulant, Pauline Martin, now Sister Agnes of Jesus.

The second factor influencing the Prioress and most of the community was that surname, Martin, and its implications. This young postulant was the third of the family to enter the Carmel of Lisieux, and unless in a convent where most or all of the nuns were saints, human nature was likely to play its customary part in discussions and decisions. The family connection must also have affected the behaviour of the three sisters themselves; the two older ones, while naturally inclined to be protective, could not be seen to favour or make excuses for Thérèse, while she was mature enough now both to want to make her own way and to let others see that she was doing so.

The conflict of attitudes in the other nuns is best seen in the behaviour of the Prioress herself. She had shown great affection for Thérèse and had supported her application for admission in spite of the regulations. On the very day when Thérèse entered, Mother Gonzague herself brought her first to the chapel, then to see the other parts of the convent, and finally to her office. There, having been told that Thérèse was reputed to know *The Imitation of Christ* by heart, she challenged the fifteen-year-old girl by selecting a chapter and asking her to recite it. The Holy Spirit may have had a say in the selection, since the chapter happened to be a favourite piece of Thérèse herself, the seventh chapter of Book Two, entitled *On Loving Jesus Above All Things*. It was the very chapter into which she had placed the little white flower picked by her father on the day when she told him formally of her desire to enter Carmel. However impressed Mother Gonzague was, she soon let the young postulant know, as Thérèse herself records in her writings, that she would not be treated otherwise than as a young applicant to the religious life who needed to be subjected to the usual tests in obedience and humiliation.

Behind this formal firmness, however, the Prioress personally continued to love and appreciate the qualities of this unusual young woman. Only a few weeks after her entry, and even while publicly and privately correcting her for even the most trivial failings, Mother Gonzague wrote about her in laudatory terms to Thérèse's aunt, Céline Guérin. When Thérèse made her vows two years later, Mother Gonzague wrote of her: 'This angelic child is only seventeen and a half years old, yet she has the judgement of someone aged thirty … she is a perfect religious.' Some years later again, she confided to another nun: 'If a prioress were to be chosen from the entire community, I would choose Sister Thérèse of the Child Jesus, in spite of her young age; she is perfect in everything.' But she added the revealing comment (by that time, Thérèse's sister, Céline, had entered Carmel after the death of their father): 'Her only fault is to have her three sisters here with her.'

At the ritual ceremony when Thérèse passed from the outside world into the convent, a spirit less prepared and determined than hers might have been dismayed by the words spoken by the person who had been most opposed to her entry, no other than Fr Delatroëtte himself. As the ecclesiastical superior, he was present at the brief ceremony *ex officio*, but he was personally a disgruntled priest whose decision regarding this young Martin girl had been set aside by the bishop; so, he could not refrain from letting this be known, even as the venerable father, Louis Martin, was offering his youngest daughter to God in the religious life, having already offered his two eldest. He declaimed formally, apparently addressing the Prioress and the nuns, but loud enough for the family and relatives to hear: 'As the appointed delegate of his lordship the bishop, I formally present to you this child of fifteen whose entry to this community you so desired. I trust she will not disappoint your hopes. And I remind you that if she does, you alone will bear the responsibility.' It was an ungracious and unpriestly declaration on such an occasion, but all present, and especially the two most concerned, Thérèse and her loving father, were already well aware of the man's attitude and they would not have expected him to behave otherwise. He intervened again two years later, when Thérèse was due to make her vows, objecting that she was too young to do so, and once more he was overruled by Bishop Hugonin, who continued to regard Thérèse with kindness, albeit embarrassing her whenever he officiated at the convent by calling her his 'dear little daughter' and retelling the story about her hair. It was only when the community was recovering from the effects of the flu epidemic, and four years after Thérèse first thwarted his authoritarian stance by entering Carmel, that Fr Delatroëtte changed his attitude towards her; he even condescended to go so far as to say that she showed great promise for the community.

CHAPTER TWELVE

A Sanctuary Disturbed

Describing that scene at the door of the convent on the day she entered Carmel, Thérèse writes: 'A few moments more, and then the door of God's Ark shut behind me, and I was being embraced by all those dear nuns who had so long been mothers to me, whose example I was to take henceforward as my rule of living. No more waiting now for the fulfilment of my ambitions; I can't tell you what a deep and refreshing sense of peace this thought carried with it. And, deep down, this sense of peace has been a lasting possession; it has never left me, even when my trials have been most severe.' Only a few lines later, she indicates the beginning of those trials: 'And yet, as you know, Mother, those first footsteps of mine brought me up against more thorns than roses ... Our Lord let me see clearly that if I wanted to win souls I would have to do it by bearing a cross; so, the more suffering came my way, the more strongly did suffering attract me.'

The sufferings she would endure were of many kinds; they began with the change in her environment from the domestic comfort of her home to the ascetic life of an enclosed religious order, change that exposed the teenage Thérèse to the basic physical suffering of cold rooms, poor food, fatigue and sleeplessness due to the severe daily routine of prayer and work. There was also, increasingly as the daily routine lengthened into months and years, the irritation and discomfort caused by being confined, however willingly for God's sake, in an enclosed convent with about two dozen other women of varying age, education, personality and social background. In the areas of religion and spirituality, Thérèse, as has been seen, had to endure for

several years, with self-effacing humility, the constant faultfind-
ing and correction that were part of the customary training in
convents. She found it difficult to confide in most of the priests
she encountered as spiritual advisers, either during retreats or
on a more permanent basis (one can spare a thought for any
priest who, dealing conscientiously with the routine spiritual
problems of the nuns, found himself suddenly confronted with
a young sister whose unique spiritual development was based
on a mind steeped in the contents of the gospels and *The
Imitation of Christ* from her girlhood and whose personal relationship with God, however simple her own presentation of it
might appear, was now on a mystical level). In her own soul, she
was to suffer from aridity in prayer and even, in her last year,
from doubts not only about salvation but even about the existence of heaven. On the very eve of her taking vows, she was suddenly distressed by the thought that she really had no vocation,
a crisis from which she was rescued firstly by the wise counsel of
her Novice-Mistress and subsequently by having her doubts
gently laughed away by the experienced Mother Gonzague.

All of these components of the cross she was to bear in pursuit of the dual purpose of her Carmelite vocation, viz. the salvation of sinners and the spiritual welfare of priests, Thérèse fore-
saw; what she could not foresee was the addition to her cross of
a suffering that had nothing to do with the religious life and that
was, because of that, perhaps more difficult to cope with than
any of the physical, social and spiritual pains and troubles within
the walls of Carmel. This was the breakdown in health, both
physical and mental, of her beloved father, the man whom she
had raised in her childish imagination, to the status of 'King of
France and Navarre'. It was a trial and a cross that would have
to be borne by all the five daughters of Louis Martin.

Throughout his life, Louis had been a healthy and vigorous
man. Even as a young man of twenty, he had gone on walking
tours in Europe and made his way, as we have seen, to the
monastery of St Bernard in the Alps where he picked that first
little white flower. It was while the family still lived at Alençon

that an incident occurred which seemed innocuous in itself but was to have unforeseen consequences. While on one of his fishing trips, Louis was bitten behind the ear by some kind of insect. This left only a black mark, but later began to show signs of infection. It continued to trouble him for years, in spite of various treatments, but whether this was the source of his later infirmities is not clear. Perhaps it had some connection with a trait in his normally benign and charitable personality about which we learn only *en passant* when, writing about the pilgrimage to Rome, Sister Thérèse says: 'Another thing I noticed about Papa was the progress in his spiritual life; like St Francis de Sales, he managed to overcome the irritability which was natural to him, and you would have said he had the sweetest temper in the world.' From this comment it is logical to deduce that the daughters of Louis Martin had seen manifestations of that 'irritability which was natural to him.'

In 1887, the year before Thérèse entered Carmel, the first sign of potentially serious trouble came when he suffered a stroke that caused some paralysis in his left side. He recovered sufficiently to take Céline and Thérèse on the tour to Rome, and in April 1888 he brought Thérèse to Carmel to join her sisters, Pauline and Marie, whom he had already generously offered to the service of God. A month later, he made an offering of another kind to the Cathedral in Lisieux. While at Mass, he heard the priest appeal for contributions towards the cost of a new altar. He inquired what the cost would be, and promptly donated the total of 10,000 francs.

Of the five daughters born to Louis and Zélie, two still remained with him. He knew that in spite of her two previous failed efforts, Léonie, the middle daughter of the five, was still considering a vocation to the religious life; but it must have come as a severe shock to this ageing and ailing man – he had already begun to suffer lapses of memory – when, just a few months after Thérèse entered Carmel, Céline told him that she, too, wished to enter there. A week later, he left home without telling anyone and did not return. He was located, four days later, by his brother-in-law, Isidore Guérin, wandering aimlessly in the streets of Le Havre. The sad news of this occurrence was brought to the three sisters in Carmel by Léonie and Céline; it would have left them with a feeling of frustration at not being able to help in caring for their father.

Louis himself must have realised that his physical condition and his mental capacities were deteriorating. He decided to set his business affairs in order, but this involved some trips to Paris and resulted in further distress for those at home when he sometimes failed to return on the appointed day and was known to be carrying large amounts of money. The date fixed for Thérèse's clothing had to be delayed because of her father's illness; but he recovered sufficiently to be present on 10 January 1889 when he led her, in the beautiful bridal dress he had supplied, to the altar in Carmel. A month later, however, his hallucinations caused him to become a danger to himself and others, and Isidore Guérin had to arrange that he be taken into care. In February 1889, he was admitted to the insane asylum at Caen, an institution housing 1,700 patients, where he would remain for the next three years. Sister Thérèse is speaking for all five sisters, in Carmel or at home, when she writes: 'I never dreamed our dear father would have to undergo such a wretched, such a humiliating experience ... I'm not going to try and describe what our feelings were; words couldn't do justice to them.'

Although being secluded in the convent meant that Thérèse, like Marie and Pauline, did not have to endure the pain of Léonie and Céline when they visited their father in Caen every week, his illness caused her to suffer a great personal disappointment when he was unable to be present for her profession and subsequent taking of the veil in September 1890. Two other absentees added minor disappointments to that major one: Bishop Hugonin had been due to preside at the ceremony and afterwards to dine with the Guérin family, but he was ill, and the Jesuit, Pére Pichon, the only spiritual director Thérèse had felt of benefit to her, had been sent to work in Canada. For the first time in years, Thérèse gave way to tears, 'which caused some astonishment,' she writes. 'I had learned by then to put up with worse set-backs without crying over them. She recovered her spiritual equilibrium quickly, and when her cousin, Jeanne Guérin, got married a week later, Thérèse decided to ask her all about the etiquette of wedding invitations. She then composed a mock but meaningful invitation to her own spiritual wedding to Jesus, as if sent from God, Our Lady, and her own parents; but, since the unnamed guests could not be present at the nuptial blessing on 8 September 1890, they are requested to be present 'tomorrow – that is, the day of eternal reckoning, when Jesus Christ, Son of God, will come on the clouds of heaven in all the splendour of his majesty to judge the living and the dead. The hour of this being still uncertain, you are asked to hold yourself in readiness and be on the watch.'

The thoughts of Sister Thérèse were turned to death and eternity soon after when she had her first experience of a death-bed. With other nuns, she assisted at the death of the aged and saintly Mother Geneviève of Saint Teresa, one of the founders of the Lisieux Carmel in 1838, who had been a model and counsellor for Thérèse from her first days in the convent. Thérèse spent two hours praying at the foot of the bed, 'telling myself that I ought to be overcome with feelings of devotion, and yet finding that it was just the other way about – I was quite numb, quite insensible. And then, at the very moment when her soul was reborn into eternity, my whole attitude changed suddenly: I was conscious of a joy and a fervour which I can't describe to you. It was just as if Mother Geneviève had communicated to me a part of the happiness she was experiencing at that moment. I find it impossible to doubt that she went straight to heaven.' Thérèse acquired an unusual relic of this holy nun, 'the last tear of a saint,' as she calls it, which she gathered on a piece of fine linen and kept 'in the little locket in which my vows are enclosed'.

When his physical condition deteriorated to the point where he was no longer able to walk, while his mental state was less agitated, it was considered that Louis Martin could be brought back to Lisieux and cared for in his own home. He came home on 10 May 1892, and a few days later Léonie and Céline brought him, in a wheelchair, to see his three daughters in Carmel. It was to be the last time they would see him. He was feeble and emaciated, emotionally distressed and hardly able to speak. That must surely have been one of the most poignant scenes ever seen in the convent. When the time came for parting, Louis gazed into his daughters' eyes and tried to gesture with his hand as if to give them a father's final blessing. He mumbled the words, 'in heaven,' and was wheeled away by Léonie and Céline while Marie, Pauline and Thérèse wept together. The family moved to a small rented house near the Guérins, and a married couple were employed to help. Louis' condition remained stable during that winter.

In February of the following year, 1893, Pauline, now aged 32, was elected Prioress in succession to Mother Gonzague who had been Prioress on several occasions in former years; however, having now completed two consecutive three-year terms, she was ineligible for election. In spite of the tension between Mother Gonzague and the two older Martin sisters, Pauline kept to the custom by which a former Prioress was appointed Novice Mistress, but she took something of a risk in then appointing Thérèse as assistant to Mother Gonzague. Now, however, Thérèse was not the young novice towards whom Mother Gonzague, while privately being fond of her, had deliberately shown formal disciplinary severity. In spite of her efforts not to attract attention, Thérèse had by now so impressed the community with her personal qualities, and especially during the recent flu epidemic, that she was described in a letter by her own former Novice Mistress, Sister Marie of the Angels, as: 'the jewel of the community'. And she continues – revealing incidentally that the image of a saintly person should not conjure up that of a boringly pious misanthrope:

> She is tall and strong, having the appearance, tone of voice, and expression of a child, that hide within her the wisdom, perfection and perspicacity of a fifty-year-old. In her soul she is always calm and in perfect control, in

everything and with everybody. She is a little innocent thing who would be allowed to receive God in holy communion without confession; but her head is full of mischief to play on anyone she pleases. She is a mystic, a comic, anything. She can make you weep when she speaks about holy things, and she can also make you burst with laughter at recreation time.

Although Mother Gonzague welcomed the appointment of Thérèse as her assistant, all the more so as she herself was now over thirty years in Carmel and suffering a deterioration in her health, Thérèse was not allowed by the Carmelite rule, because she had two sisters in the community, to have any official position or title, or to play any part in community elections or legislation. But while she humbly requested that she be known simply as 'senior novice', she effectively fulfilled the role of Novice Mistress for the four and a half years that were left of her life, Mother Gonzague confidently leaving the task to the young nun whose qualities were already causing even some of the older nuns to come to her for counsel.

Thérèse was also asked by her sister, Pauline, as Prioress, to take charge of the art work in the convent. She had no formal training, but had always been interested in sketching and painting. At Pauline's request, she painted a fresco in the oratory. Another talent was set in motion when one of the nuns asked her to write a poem about Mary and Jesus. She did so, entitling the poem *The Divine Dew* and using her favourite metaphor of the flower, this time a rose. Although Pauline considered that she should concentrate on painting rather than poetry, Thérèse continued to write poems, at the request of other nuns or as a gift on their feastdays, but also to give lyrical expression to her own spiritual emotions. Up to the time of her death, she had composed over fifty poems, to musical airs, intending them to be sung like hymns.

Thérèse also branched into drama. The novices were expected to provide an entertainment for the community at Christmas, and it was for this that Thérèse composed her first play, about her childhood heroine, Jeanne d'Arc, in which she delighted the community by her acting in the title role. She went on to write eight such plays altogether, also directing, designing and sometimes acting. But she was already becoming aware of sinister signs in her health, consisting of bouts of weakness, with chest pains and persistent coughs. Her cousin, Jeanne Guérin, had married a doctor, Francis La Néele, and at her request, and probably having consulted her father, Isidore, a professional pharmacist, he prescribed some medication which, whatever its immediate palliative effect, would proved of little curative value.

The continuing worry of the three sisters in Carmel about their stricken father was further heightened when they learned, in June 1893, that Léonie, ever the unpredictable one of the five, was going to Caen to enter the Visitation Convent for the second time. This departure must have made a further deleterious impact on the already distressed Louis; it also left Céline on her own to care for their father, although she had the constant support of the Guérin family along with the married couple who had been hired. The Guérins had recently inherited, with another family, a large property called *La Musse*, near Evreux. Léonie and Céline had enjoyed holidays there with the Guérins. With the help of Desiré, the hired man, Céline and her cousin, Marie Guérin, were able to bring Louis to Evreux where he showed great delight in the scenery and in the song of the birds, as well as in the talent of Marie Guérin when she sang and played the piano. After surviving the winter, spent back in Lisieux, he suffered a heart attack in May 1894, but recovered sufficiently to be taken again to Evreux in July with the Guérins and Céline. While there, however, he suffered another heart attack and received the Last Sacraments. He died on Sunday 29 July 1894. His body was taken back to Lisieux where he was buried on 2 August after a Requiem Mass in the Cathedral. It was a further blast of desolation from the outside world to the three sisters in Carmel that they could not be present at the Requiem Mass or at the burial of their beloved father.

Only a week after the death of Louis Martin, Céline requested entry into Carmel. Her sister, Pauline, was now Prioress, but the reaction of the convent's ecclesiastical superior, Fr Delatroëtte, to the prospect of a fourth Martin sister in a community of less than thirty nuns was predictably hostile. The community themselves, however, apart from one or two, were in favour, possibly influenced as much by the growing reputation of Sister Thérèse as by the approval of the former Prioress, Mother Gonzague. Pauline had been torn between the desire to join her sisters in Carmel and the invitation from Pére Pichon SJ, to go to Canada where he wanted her to found a new secular institute.

Thérèse, of course, had prayed that her childhood family soulmate would become her spiritual sister in Carmel, and the modern reader will certainly find it quaint to read the extreme spiritual measures she took in pursuance of her pious wish:

> ... the thought that she might give herself to an earthly husband just couldn't find room in my mind ... I remember one day when I knew she was going out to an evening party, and it worried me so much that the tears came to my eyes, a thing which wasn't usual with me now, and I entreated our Lord to see that she didn't dance. My prayer was heard. In the ordinary way, she was an accomplished dancer, but that evening she found it impossible, and the partner who was in attendance on her simply couldn't get her to take the floor. There was nothing for it but to take her back to her place, and there, in some embarrassment, he left her, and didn't come back the whole evening.

And who could blame the poor chap? But Saint Thérèse would surely ask us now to consider charitably that she had entered Carmel at the age of fifteen, and also that her prayers were not directed at ruining the evening for Céline's partner but at protecting the vocation which she firmly believed God had instilled in her sister's soul. We learn from other sources, however, that Céline, a vivacious and attractive young woman of twenty-five, had also been considering a marriage proposal from a young lawyer who was very much in love with her.

Céline entered Carmel in September 1894. While it must have been a cause of great joy to her sisters to welcome her to that haven where they hoped she would share their peace of mind and soul after the harrowing years she had spent in caring for their father, they could not foresee that her joining them would make it possible for the powers of evil to subject them to a disturbance of that haven very different from the familial anguish they had shared with Céline and Léonie during the long agony of their father.

CHAPTER THIRTEEN

The Vanishing Woman

When Céline Martin arrived at the Carmel of Lisieux in September 1894, she brought with her more than the normal trousseau a girl aspiring to be the spiritual bride of Christ would be expected to provide (this was one of the considerations preventing Bernadette Soubirous in Lourdes from pursuing her desire to be a nun, until the sisters at the hospice removed that obstacle by providing her with what was necessary). Some household items, like a clock, were apparently deemed a welcome addition to the furnishings of the poor convent; another item was a special source of joy to Thérèse; this was the statue of Our Lady, known now as 'Our Lady of the Smile', that had been central to the sudden cure of her mysterious illness as a child. In the following weeks and months, Thérèse often knelt in prayer before it, and she would later gaze at it lovingly as she lay dying.

An item that was neither furniture nor religious would have been an object of fascination to the whole community. From childhood, Céline had shown a talent for drawing and painting (it will be remembered that her father, Louis, had offered to send her to Paris for training). Later, she took up the study of the new art of photography and became proficient even to the extent of developing her own photographs. Although Bernadette Soubirous had been photographed in Lourdes in 1858 by some early practitioners, photography was still a complicated and expensive procedure and the camera was a large and cumbersome appliance. The arrival of such an item in that enclosed Carmelite convent must have been as exciting as the gift of a computer would be nowadays to some poor convent in the third world. Céline Martin became one of the first people to photograph life in a convent. Among many other images, she has left over forty photos of her younger sister, Thérèse, in groups with the community, at recreation, at work such as laundry or haymaking, and alone, posed in various places. The last poignant photos of Thérèse show her, a month before her death, lying ill in bed in the cloister, and finally, robed once more in the Carmelite habit and adorned with a chaplet of flowers, Thérèse in death, lying in her coffin beneath her beloved statue of 'Our Lady of the Smile.'

An item of special personal interest to Thérèse in her spiritual life was a notebook Céline brought with her. This contained quotations from the Old Testament, copied by Céline from a Bible in the home of Uncle Isidore Guérin. Apparently, Catholics then, as in times before and since, if they read Holy Scripture in private at all, were more familiar with the New Testament. Thérèse, to her surprise and delight, found that the image of God portrayed in the Old Testament was not always that of the just but retributive judge. Images of a loving and merciful parent were also to be found in plenty. Even the image of the Good Shepherd used by Jesus himself had been used long before in the Book of Isaiah: 'God shall feed his flock like a shepherd; he shall gather together the lambs with his arm, and shall take them up in his bosom.' These new insights helped in the continuing development of her Little Way of holiness, the path in which she was now training the novices and towards which she was counselling even some of the other nuns.

A more modern image gave her another angle from which to approach her concept of a loving God eager to respond with grace and mercy to the slightest request from a loving soul. In the expensive hotel where Louis and his daughters stayed during the visit to Rome, the young Thérèse had seen the wonderful invention called a lift that eliminated the labour of climbing one or more flights of stairs. The painstaking step by step advance up the stairway of perfection, always with the danger of slipping or falling by reason of human failing coupled with the insidious ploys of the envious devil, was the common image used by many spiritual writers. Thérèse added the modern image of the lift to the biblical one she had already used so often, that of a loving father stooping to take his little child in his arms. Any soul following her Little Way of love and confidence would not have to labour step by painful step, in fear of a God ever on the watch for failure, but would be raised by our loving Father in heaven to a new level of hope and joy in God's mercy.

In her convent library, Thérèse would have read the former writers on the spiritual life, including her own patron, St Teresa of Avila (1513-1582), reformer of the Carmelites and described by a renowned historian of Spanish literature, Professor Fitzmaurice-Kelly, as probably 'the greatest woman who ever handled a pen, the single one of all her sex who stands beside the world's great masters'. She was aware that her own approach to the spiritual life, although based solidly on the gospel and on long-approved works like *The Imitation of Christ*, could be wrongly interpreted and regarded as simplistic or naïve. In fact, she herself addressed this danger on one occasion. One of her novices, Sister Marie of the Trinity, who seems to have been the most responsive to her guidance, told her that she would like to pass on some of Thérèse's spiritual counsel to her own parents. The response of Sister Thérèse was to warn her to be very careful in doing so, 'because our Little Way, if misunderstood, could be taken for quietism or illuminism. You must not think,' she went on, 'that to follow the path of love means to follow the path of repose, full of sweetness and consolations. It is exactly the opposite. To offer oneself as a victim to Love means to give oneself up without any reservations for whatever God pleases, which means to expect to share with Jesus his humiliations, his chalice of bitterness.'

That is a significant insight into the true meaning of the Little Way of St Thérèse. There are probably some among her prejudiced atheistic or irreligious critics, people who dismiss her as just a sentimental and childish pious nun, who would need to consult the dictionary to find the meaning of those terms, quietism and illuminism, in their historic and theological context; there are others who might think that the 'Little Way' of Thérèse is some kind of amenable and more accommodating spirituality than revealed religion, with its dogmatic beliefs, sacraments, commandments and devotions. Thérèse would insist, like her English contemporary, John Henry Newman, probably the greatest religious intellect of the nineteenth century, that there can be no true religion without dogma and commandments. She would have little regard for the cosy types of vague spirituality that have become popular in modern secularist societies because they impose no obligation other than a reciprocal philanthropy along with a regard for nature that is more a tribute to Pan than to a divine Creator.

Like many of the potentially beneficial products of the blighted genius of *homo sapiens* – the man who made the first bow and arrow killed an animal before he killed another human being, and the scientists who split the atom did not see the mushroom cloud over Hiroshima in their microscopes – the camera was no sooner developed, as man's ingenious mechanical attempt to replicate the mystifying eye fashioned by the omnipotent originator of all species from the fly to man, than it was being used and abused. While those very first photographs of Bernadette Soubirous were being sold in France, tourists in Paris were also being offered the first provocative photos of women. In our own time, those truly amazing developments, film and television, undreamt of by the users of the primitive cameras, continue to demonstrate, on an even more universal and socially pervasive scale, the moral good or evil that can result from any human invention.

Thus it was that the strange appliance brought into the Carmel at Lisieux, while adding some unexpected moments of delight and joy to the rigours of life in that enclosed convent, became the means of an unintended development that brought grief and annoyance to disturb the peace of that holy sanctuary. Although she had her younger sister, Thérèse, as unofficial Novice Mistress and familial counsellor, the twenty-five-year old Céline Martin did not adapt very readily to the change from her comfortable secular life to the rules and rigours of Carmel;

but she joined enthusiastically in the artistic activities of Thérèse. She was an intelligent and cultured young woman, gifted artistically, and her talents were put to good use in the production of the plays being written by Thérèse. Shortly after Céline's entry, Thérèse wrote a play about her heroine, Joan of Arc, entitled *Joan of Arc Accomplishing her Mission*. The production almost fulfilled Thérèse's life-long wish for martyrdom, but in a uniquely dramatic manner, when the set caught fire while Thérèse, in the title role, was bound to the stake. Céline helped to quench the flames and calm the more elderly members of the audience. A year later, in June 1896, in spite of her failing health, Thérèse wrote another play, *The Triumph of Humility*. This was inspired by the report in the newspapers of the extraordinary conversion from Freemasonry and Satanism of a young woman named Diana Vaughan.

In the nineteenth century, Freemasonry, especially in France and Italy, was to the Catholic Church what Communism would be in the twentieth century. Communism, however, was an open and visible enemy, whereas Freemasonry, being a secret oath-bound society, could exert its anti-Catholic, and sometimes anti-social, even revolutionary, policies through its members placed high and low in all walks of life. Its very secrecy allows Masons to defend it as a harmless friendly society, otherwise how could people like King George VI of England have been a member, as well as the Archbishop of Canterbury and half of the Anglican bishops of England in the twentieth century? In the context of that particular discussion, it is of interest to quote from a letter in the Anglican *Church Times* (30 March, 1951) in which an Anglican clergyman wrote: 'It has been seriously suggested that if I wish to get on in the church I ought to become a Freemason; and numerous Episcopal instances have been quoted!' In the matter of Masonic membership today, anywhere and in any walk of life, it is true to say – it being a secret, oath-bound society – only God knows.

With regard to its effect on society as a whole, historians ascribe the French Revolution of 1789, and other such events in

Europe, to the subversive influence of Masonry. Ironically, although the first literally free masons are thought by some scholars to have been the anonymous craftsmen who executed the artistic stonework on the great Catholic cathedrals of the Middle Ages, in its modern form of lodges, as organised in London in the early eighteenth century, Freemasonry, especially in France and Italy, was virulently anti-Catholic, even anti-religious. From the first condemnation by Pope Clement XII in 1738, Freemasonry has been condemned by nine popes. In 1884, Pope Leo XIII, the pope at whose feet Thérèse had knelt, issued his Encyclical, *Humanum Genus*, in which he declared Freemasonry to be utterly incompatible with the Christian religion, and forbade Catholics, as they valued their faith and eternal salvation, to join it.

It may surprise some lovers of the music of the greatest genius of that art to learn that Wolfgang Amadeus Mozart became a Mason in Vienna in 1784 – he was later admitted to the grade of Master – and even composed music specially for performance at Masonic rituals and gatherings. It in no way lessens our enjoyment of operas like *The Magic Flute* and *The Marriage of Figaro* to learn that they are redolent, respectively, of Masonic ritual and socialist political views, nor does it deter the present Pope, Benedict XVI, a talented classical pianist, from declaring the genius of Salzburg to be the cultural influence that 'thoroughly penetrated our souls' as he grew up in rural Bavaria. 'His music,' the Pope has said, 'is not just entertainment; it contains the whole tragedy of human existence.' Mozart also, of course, composed more than sixty pieces of sacred music, including some of the most famous Masses – I myself acknowledge a personal debt for one of the most moving musical experiences of my life when, at an ordinary Mass in St Peter's in Rome, a visiting German choir assembled near the altar sang Mozart's motet, *Ave Verum*.

While the ambivalence of Mozart's Masonic and Catholic beliefs must remain a puzzle, it is not surprising that Pope Benedict is reputed to include some Mozart when he seeks a little

daily solace at the piano from the cares of the human race. Nor
was it surprising for the Catholics of France when Pope Leo XIII
took a special interest in the case of a notorious French journalist
named Léo Taxil who had made a reputation for himself as a
Freemason by publishing over one hundred anti-Catholic pam-
phlets in a series with the unsubtle title, *Anticlerical Library*, and
with a newspaper of his own, closely related in title and content,
l'Anticlérical. He was also the author of some scurrilous books,
including a mocking life of Jesus, a similarly flippant book on
the Bible, and best-sellers such as *The Debaucheries of a Confessor*
and *The Pope's Mistresses*. In 1879, after he published another
anti-Catholic volume, even the anti-clerical authorities had to
charge him, in response to protests from Catholics, with 'insult-
ing a religion recognised by the State.' He was, of course, duly
acquitted.

Having been expelled from the Freemasons in 1882, for reasons unknown, he made a public declaration of conversion to
the Catholic faith and was solemnly received into the church.
Finding himself penniless, he next turned his talents in the other
direction and published a book entitled *Confessions d'un libre
penseur (Confessions of a freethinker)* which went through forty-
five editions – both Catholic and non-Catholic readers were
eager to hear his two sides of the religious controversy. He then
embarked on a series of pamplets, books and articles – and, inevitably, even a Catholic newspaper – attacking Freemasonry
with the same sarcasm and mockery with which he had previously attacked Catholicism; even more significant was his sensational revelation of what he said were the secret rituals and im-
moral practices of the Freemasons.

The notorious Leo Taxil's *volte face* writings inevitably became
a welcome and fruitful source of material for Catholic authorities and journalists. In 1887 he had an audience with Pope Leo
XIII, whose encyclical against Freemasonry had been written the
previous year. The Pope praised Taxil's anti-Masonic books,
saying that he had them in his library, and he bestowed on their
author a special blessing and commendation. After some years,

Taxil produced an even more sensational item in the story of a young woman named Diana Vaughan who had converted to the Catholic faith from Freemasonry through the intercession of the heroine of France, Jeanne d'Arc. He published the revelations supplied to him by this convert, including lurid accounts of the satanic sexual orgies in which she had engaged with Satan himself in various grotesque manifestations. When Diana announced, through Taxil, her representative with the public, that she was now offering herself to God as a victim to be punished appropriately for her repulsive and heinous sins, her reputation as a modern Jeanne d'Arc was enhanced. Léo Taxil also published her pious hymns and prayers, including a eucharistic novena that impressed even the Pope, and a hymn to Jeanne d'Arc that was sung not only in France but even in some churches in Rome.

In the Carmel of Lisieux, as in every convent in France, the name of Diana Vaughan became revered as that of a modern Jeanne d'Arc braving the fury of the Freemasons and other anti-Catholic forces. Uncle Isidore Guérin, whose daughter, Marie, had joined her cousins in Carmel in August 1895, having sold his pharmacy business, had taken some work as a journalist with a Catholic paper, and he was the obvious source from which the news about Diana, as well as copies of her writings and those of her protector, Leo Taxil, came to the nuns. To Sister Thérèse, in particular, Diana Vaughan must have seemed an inspiring figure, a soulmate in her devotion to Jeanne d'Arc and in her offering of herself to God as a victim. The Eucharistic Novena of Diana, which had impressed the Pope himself, must have been read and discussed in every convent in France. Sister Thérèse found it so inspiring that she copied passages from it. She also expressed a fervent wish for Diana: 'My greatest desire would be to see her united with Jesus in our little Carmel,' a sentiment which, one source says, 'delighted the entire community.' When Mother Agnes suggested that Thérèse might write a poem for Diana, however, no poetic inspiration came, but Thérèse wrote to Diana (c/o Léo Taxil) and enclosed a photograph taken by Céline which showed Thérèse as Jeanne d'Arc chained in prison, with Céline as St Catherine, one of Joan's heavenly 'voices', in a scene from Thérèse's play, *Joan of Arc Accomplishing Her Mission*, produced in the convent the previous year. Thérèse was also inspired to write a second play about Jeanne d'Arc, *The Triumph of Humility*, in which the evil spirits are given the same names Diana had used in her eucharistic novena.

When Diana replied, thanking Thérèse with pious appreciation for the gift of the photograph, the letter was probably read aloud to the community, and re-read by Thérèse and other nuns individually, as a valuable spiritual document. Meanwhile, since the first news of her conversion two years ago, the reputation of Diana Vaughan as an apologist for the Catholic Faith and an opponent of its anti-clerical detractors had increased to the extent that the Vatican, now more cautious, decided to set up a commission to examine her conversion and the orthodoxy of her writings. The initial findings of these inquiries began to raise doubts and misgivings. There were already some voices, both clerical and lay, raising doubts. One such was the Catholic Bishop of Charleston in America, a city linked by Diana Vaughan with her satanic past. His open scepticism had earned him a rebuke from a Vatican source. Another hostile critic was the Vicar-Apostolic of Gibraltar who rejected as utter nonsense the claim in Diana's revelations that under the Rock of Gibraltar there was a huge satanic forge where the instruments of Masonic ritual and orgies were manufactured.

The crucial question as to why Diana Vaughan had not made any public appearances had always been credibly answered by Léo Taxil, citing the danger to which she would have been exposed from the anti-Catholic elements whose fury she had aroused by her revelations, as well as the harassment she would endure from curious crowds and from journalists. She had been obliged, it was explained, to stay secluded, *incognito*, in various convents. When the demands from both supporters and opponents became so pressing that such plausible explanations were no longer sufficient to silence them, Léo Taxil finally announced that he would bring Diana Vaughan to be seen at a public lecture to be given by him on April 19 1897.

In a large hall in Paris on that day, before an invited audience of several hundred, including some priests and monks as well as noted Freemasons and anti-clerical journalists, Léo Taxil made the astounding announcement that there was no such person as the anti-Masonic convert, Diana Vaughan, with all her startling revelations about satanism and Freemasonry. She and her writings were all an invention of his own. He had employed a young Protestant Frenchwoman – more a freethinker than a Protestant, he asserted – who was a professional typist and the representative of an American typewriter company, and who gladly allowed him to use her own name in the hoax, to type up his original scripts and copy out personal letters by hand. He had also recruited a willing accomplice in the form of a much-travelled friend who, at first unaware, and gradually made fully aware of the nature and extent of the anti-Catholic hoax, was able to supply authentic background material for some of Taxil's (or Diana's) fabrications about Masonry in its non-European manifestations. He also bombastically revealed that his twelve-year hoax, with which he had humiliatingly fooled the Pope and the faithful, was only the latest in a series of such brilliantly-conceived deceptions. Previously, he claimed, he had made people believe that the harbour in his native Marseilles was infested by sharks, with the result that a naval ship had been sent to find and destroy those non-existent predators. He had also announced the discovery of an ancient underwater city in Lake Geneva, a hoax which brought tourists and archaeologists flocking there, some of them adding their own shadowy sightings to Taxil's concocted version of submerged ruins.

The reaction of the audience in that hall in Paris was predictable. For different reasons, both the Freemasons and the Catholics, lay or religious, joined in shouts of anger and disgust, while some of the atheists just enjoyed the show and applauded. What all in the audience saw was the backdrop to the lecture, a large copy of the photograph sent to Diana Vaughan by Sister

Thérèse. To this, Taxil made several mocking references about the credulity of the simple-minded nuns who had sent it to him, without descending to the depth of actually naming them. He also ridiculed the credulous old Pope in Rome along with the Catholic clergy and journalists whom he had duped over a period of twelve years.

Having enjoyed his moment of glory, Léo Taxil needed police protection to escape to the safety of a nearby café; he then faded into the deeper safety of obscurity and died in 1907. While his sensational lecture, with its mockery of the Catholic faith, is still used in Masonic circles and propaganda, the impact of his sensational revelations on the church in general was eventually no more than that of the many similar pebbles that have been aimed at the Rock on which Christ founded the church to which he made the divine promise that the powers of hell would never prevail against it and that he would be with it until the end of time. He also, of course, warned that the church would be the object of persecution and the butt of ridicule from the powers of evil.

The effect of Taxil's hoax on that enclosed convent in Lisieux, however, was more concentrated and immediate than its ephemeral ripple on the waters on which the barque of Peter sails to its eternal destiny. We can only try to feel that effect by imagining ourselves seated with the nuns in the Carmel of Lisieux when they first heard – we are in a world before radio or television could bring instantaneous news into every home from all over the world – that Diana Vaughan had vanished from the face of the earth, had never even existed. No more needs to be said. Thérèse, we are told, took the letter she had received from Diana Vaughan, tore it into shreds, and threw it on the compost heap in the convent garden. She, and the community in shocked sympathy with her, never mentioned the name of Diana Vaughan again. Nor is there any mention of that name, or of the whole episode, in the autobiographical *Story of a Soul*. Although we can believe how Sister Thérèse would have added the name of Leo Taxil to her prayer-list of special candidates for God's loving mercy, the personal humiliation, added to the shock to her religious sensibility, of having been personally and publicly involved with so devious and malevolent an atheist, must have caused further suffering to a soul already struggling with the particular problems, unknown to the common flock, which test the faith and perseverance of souls singled out by God as candidates for saintliness and mystical experience.

Apart from the fact that subsequent inquiries – why were they not made much earlier? – came up with some interesting revelations concerning Léo Taxil himself, such as that, having been born in Marseilles in 1854, he was christened Marie Joseph Gabriel Antoine – indicating a Catholic family – was registered under the elegantly hyphenated surname, Jogand-Pagès, and that his first recorded achievements in adult life were as a deserter and a thief, the question remains: how was an atheistic author like Leo Taxil able to compose prayers, letters and books so piously orthodox and devotional in their content, and to use these in an elaborate hoax that for years duped the authorities and faithful of the Catholic Church? Undoubtedly, the man must have been brilliant in his own right, but readers who believe that the Spirit of Evil is something more than a metaphor for the vile behaviour of human beings will consider that the concocted sensational revelations of Leo Taxil concerning satanism were in themselves an indication that the entire episode of his Diana Vaughan anti-Catholic hoax was itself the product of the machinations of a deposed and malignant archangel, using a human intelligence to pursue its ever-futile rebellion against its own and humanity's Creator. That is the lesson of the Book of Job, the dramatic masterpiece of the Old Testament, itself the inspiration for some modern literary works such as the Pulitzer Prize winning play, *JB*, by Archibald Macleish, and the novel, *The Only Problem*, by Muriel Spark. In Job, the ancient author imagines God and Satan playing their parts in the supernatural sections, while Job and his wife, with the logical but unhelpful comforting friends, are the human beings trying, with the resources of our limited human reason, to understand the mysteries of pain and suffering.

To the daily sacrifices to which she was now long accustomed, to the physical torments of increasing ill-health and the spiritual agony of aridity in prayer and spiritual desolation, Thérèse could now add the unique personal suffering resulting from the embarrassment and humiliation of her innocent involvement in the affair of the vanishing woman.

CHAPTER FOURTEEN

Through Agony to Glory

Although Thérèse had been suffering from a persistent sore throat for a few years previously, and her Uncle Isidore Guérin had expressed concern about her health, it was not until Holy Week in 1896 that she received the first ominous sign of the early death she had herself predicted. On the morning of Good Friday, she saw that the warm liquid she had felt gurgling from her throat during the night was her own blood. From then on, until her death on 30 September the following year, she was to suffer the physical deterioration and increasing pain associated with tuberculosis. It was a disease that claimed many thousands of victims every year, many of them young and healthy until struck down by this scourge that would destroy their lungs and waste away their bodies almost to a skeleton. A few months after that first hemoptyses caused Thérèse to realise that her own days were numbered, one of the other nuns, Sister Marie Antoinette, died of tuberculosis. Others would die of it in the years after Thérèse's death, including her cousin and childhood friend, Marie Guérin, daughter of Uncle Isidore, the professional pharmacist. Marie had entered Carmel in 1895, and had been, as a novice, under the spiritual tutelage of Thérèse; she died in 1905. There was no effective treatment for tuberculosis until antibiotics were discovered nearly half a century later.

The prolonged physical agony that ended in her death was only one aspect of the many ways in which God accepted the formal Act of Immolation made by Thérèse when she offered herself as a loving victim to Jesus for the salvation of sinners. Only two days after that warning on Good Friday in 1896, she entered into a spiritual agony in which her faith in heaven and the next life were to be subjected to mental trials so severe that she was afraid to discuss them, even with her blood sisters, in any but a general reference lest her personal spiritual torments should undermine the faith of others. The aridity in prayer that had often troubled her severely did not leave her. She had already recorded her difficulty, in spite of her lifelong devotion to Our Lady expressed in many poems and prayers, of keeping her mind on the Mysteries of the Rosary – a consolation to us ordinary souls – and how she found no help in the many finely-phrased prayers contained in holy books; her resort in that latter difficulty was to recite very slowly the Our Father and the Hail Mary, an exercise that can be recommended to saint or sinner and that can, by God's grace, make us aware of the soul-shaking import of those two extraordinary prayers, prayers that are usually rattled off with the prattling non-meditative recitative learned in our childhood. What prayers composed by human minds, no matter how fervent or poetic, can excel the one composed and taught to his disciples by Our divine Lord, Jesus Christ himself, and the other formed from the salvific words of the Angel Gabriel, the Virgin Mary, and the church?

In these last months of her life, Thérèse also took up her pen again to continue the story of her spiritual life in response to the order given her by Mother Marie de Gonzague, elected Prioress once more in 1896 – Thérèse expressed surprise and disappointment that her sister, Pauline, was not elected for the second three-year period as allowed by the rules. She also continued to fulfil vicariously her desire to be a missionary and spread the good news of Christ to the world. While Pauline was still Prioress, a young seminarian had written to the convent in Lisieux asking that one of the sisters make him the special object of her prayers for priests. Aware of the great love of the missions in her young sister, Pauline chose Thérèse for the role. Now Mother de Gonzague asked Thérèse to take on a second 'spiritual brother' who had requested the same back-up source of grace for his work in the missions. Thérèse carried on a correspondence with both of them in which further insights into her own holiness and spiritual wisdom are to be found.

As her illness progressed, Thérèse became unable to do any physical work and even had to withdraw from the community prayers and recreation. She continued to write as long as she could, and she recorded honestly, and with her indomitable humour, some of the small but persistently irritating trials that were a test of her love, for God's sake, of her sisters in religion – she instanced the nun who, kneeling behind her in the oratory, used to make a clicking noise with her teeth; another nun who splashed Thérèse with her vigorous efforts during the communal laundry sessions, and the arthritic and cranky old nun who accepted Thérèse's help but snapped complaints at her. One trial that caused Thérèse a special effort in charity was intellectual rather than physical – she felt a surge of annoyance whenever some other nun, to whom she had revealed a striking thought or some spiritual insight, brought this out in general conversation later without acknowledging its source. Thérèse described this as 'mental theft', akin to the physical loss she felt when someone appropriated a lamp or any other object without asking her. She recognised the insidious temptation to pride in her reaction to this particular annoyance – she always reminded her novices that pride is the first and most dangerous of the seven deadly sins – and she overcame it by silent prayer; but anyone who has had to endure a similar experience, even in the common intercourse of social or pub conversation, will know how irritating it can be.

It was in the midst of all this suffering, physical, spiritual and mental, that the humiliation of mockery involved in the revelation of the Leo Taxil hoax came as a totally unexpected and shattering intrustion into the life of Sister Thérèse, a highly intelligent and sensitive, but physically weakened and mentally tormented young nun. It was part of the passion of Thérèse as it had been of Our Divine Saviour himself – as he hung on the Cross, the humiliation of mockery was added by his enemies to the physical torture of flagellation and crucifixion. When she was finally confined to the convent infirmary, on 8 July 1897, Sister Thérèse had just over two months more to live. Her final

sufferings are catalogued in medical reports that make grue-
some reading, as well as in the personal accounts of her family
and religious sisters. Dying of tuberculosis is not an easy death.
As evidence of this, I ask the charity of my readers in recording a
personal emotional memory: I was present at the death-bed of
my sister, Lily, when our family watched her die of tuberculosis
at the same age as Sister Thérèse.

Even now, during her last days on earth, and in the midst of
her torments, physical and spiritual, Thérèse kept the promise
she had made at her profession, to pray for sinners and priests.
When she received Holy Communion for the last time, on 19
August, 1897 – she was physically unable to do so again up to her
death on 30 September – that day happening to be the feast of St
Hyacinth, she offered the Holy Communion especially for a man
of that name, Hyacinth Loyson, who for many years had been officially an object of scandal and obloquy to the Carmelites of
France and Europe. He had been a Carmelite priest, with a reputation as a scholar and preacher, a personal friend of John Henry
Newman and other intellectuals, and had risen to be Provincial
of the Discalced Carmelites. However, like others of his kind ever
since Christ founded his church and selected a man to be his
Vicar on Earth, Fr Loyson's intellectual opinions were stronger
than his faith. In 1869, when Thérèse Martin was still a child of
four, he left the church because of his disagreement with papal
infallibility (proclaimed as an Article of Faith a year later). He
then, like Luther, married and founded a church of his own (his
wife was an American Protestant widow who converted to his
version of the church and bore him a son). His name was pro-
scribed in all Carmels, but ever since hearing about him after her
entrance to Carmel, Thérèse had kept him in her prayers, referring to him always as her 'brother' just as she spoke about the
young priests with whom she corresponded. Loyson never repented publicly, but when, some years after the death of Thérèse,
Céline sent him some of her sister's poems, along with a copy of
The Story of a Soul, he replied and thanked her, saying that he was
very moved by the book and by Thérèse's concern for him.

THE ONE WHO HID AWAY

Her sisters, Pauline and Marie and Céline, as well as her cousin, Marie Guérin, were among those who cared for Thérèse and watched by her bedside in her final days; they also, especially Pauline, Mother Agnes of Jesus, recorded every word she spoke up to her final moments; some of this material was added to the original version of *The Story of a Soul,* and it was published separately later when *The Story of a Soul* had made the outside world aware of the little saint who had lived and died as a member of that small community of nuns, unknown to the great world of humanity, dedicating their lives to prayer and sacrifice for the benefit of humanity.

These *Last Conversations,* comprising brief spiritual observations as well as the exclamations of a woman suffering excruciating pain, are naturally more spontaneous and fragmentary than the material in the three manuscripts that went to the making of *The Story of a Soul.* To those who may have imagined that saints must surely die a peaceful death as they pass into the presence of the God they have loved and served on earth, some of the utterances of Thérèse in her last days will come as a surprise. She once whispered that the pain was 'enough to drive one out of one's mind.' On another occasion, to the nuns watching and praying, she said: 'My sisters, pray for the poor sick who are dying. If you only knew what happens! How little it takes to lose one's patience! You must be kind towards all of them without exception ... Oh, how good God will have to be so that I can bear all I'm suffering. Never would I have believed I could suffer so much. And yet I believe I'm not at the end of my pains; but he will not abandon me.' But perhaps the most revealing of those deathbed comments was something she said to her sister, Pauline, a few days before she died – and Mother Agnes of Jesus must have felt alarm in her own soul as she jotted down these words: 'Watch carefully, Mother, when you will have patients a prey to violent pains; don't leave near them any medicines that are poisonous. I assure you, it needs only a second, when one suffers intensely, to lose one's reason. Then one could easily poison oneself.' Later, she added: 'Oh yes! What a grace it is to have faith! If I had not had any faith, I would have committed suicide without an instant's hesitation.' There is much material for thought and discussion in those words of a dying saint. Mother Agnes (Pauline) herself was so upset and shaken that she went away to pray for Thérèse before a statue of the Sacred Heart.

At her bedside Thérèse had the gospels and *The Imitation of Christ*, the two sources of her spiritual growth from the infancy of her innocent soul, as well as two of the works of St John of the Cross, the Carmelite friar who had initiated her into the mystical way of divine love. Thérèse died on 30 September 1897. In her last moments, she raised her emaciated body from the bed and cried out, 'My God, I love you!' 'Suddenly,' we are told, 'she raised her eyes and her face became very beautiful. She looked for a long time at the statue of the Blessed Virgin, then fell back, her eyes closed, with a mysterious smile on her lips.' Her sister, Céline, photographed that smiling face in death.

As if by a providential foresight, Sister Thérèse could not be buried in the convent burial plot. It was deemed by the municipal authorities of Lisieux to be already too full. Uncle Isidore had recently bought a plot in the town cemetery, and it was here that Thérèse was buried on 4 October 1894. Her sisters in Carmel were unable to be present, but her sister, Léonie, now a member of the Visitation sisters at Caen, led the small group of thirty people up the hill from the local church to the cemetery. If she had been buried in the cemetery of the enclosed Carmel, the grave of Sister Thérèse, not being accessible to the public, could not have been visited by the ever-increasing number of pilgrims who came to pray there as soon as *The Story of a Soul* began to circulate widely. In 1923, on the occasion of her beatification, her remains were transferred to the chapel in Carmel.

What happened next, as the saying goes, is history. I have described in the opening chapters how the publication of *The Story of a Soul* made known to the outside world the life and holiness of a young woman whose only wish from her girlhood had been to hide herself away from the world in a life of prayer and sacrifice for that world. But even when people began to come to pray at her grave, and an increasing stream of letters began to arrive at the Carmel of Lisieux telling of favours attributed to the Carmelite nun who had promised to 'spend my heaven in doing good on earth' and 'I will send a shower of roses', the idea that Thérèse might be canonised officially, as she was already being done unofficially by the ancient *vox populi* method, did not occur even to some of those who had known her personally. Apparently, the traditional stereotype of a candidate for sainthood implied great public achievement in the cause of God, or spectacular martyrdom, or the founding of a new religious order. That was not the impressive image conjured up by the somewhat rambling and piecemeal autobiography of a pious young nun who simply lived quietly in her convent and wrote down some spiritual thoughts of her own about the love of God, while describing herself poetically as just a little flower that Jesus might pick.

Uncle Isidore Guérin, who had financed the publication of the first edition of 2,000 copies of *The Story of a Soul*, was among those who were surprised by the proposal that his niece should be considered a candidate for sainthood; if she were, he said, many other nuns, including his own daughter, Marie, who had died of tuberculosis in 1905, should also be considered for that honour. He was especially annoyed by reports of miracles connected with the name of Thérèse. Uncle Isidore, brother-in-law of Louis Martin, had been a stalwart supporter of the Martin girls since the death of his sister, Zélie, when Thérèse was only four years old, and after the tragic illness and death of their father, but he probably still retained the image of Thérèse as the pampered baby of the family and as a sentimental and unpractical girl, and her account of her life might have appeared to him to be just a collection of childhood anecdotes interspersed with some rather pious meditations.

The new Bishop of Bayeux suspected that it was the Martin sisters in Carmel who were behind the move to initiate an investigation into the holiness of Thérèse; but perhaps the most unexpected reaction came from Léonie Martin, now Sister

Françoise-Thérèse in the Convent of the Visitation at Caen. It is recorded that she was in the convent garden hanging out laundry when her Superior came out to tell her that there was talk of beginning a process for the canonisation of her sister. Léonie dismissed the idea, saying, 'Thérèse was very kind, but a saint? Really!' and went on hanging the clothes. It was only when the learned theologians began to study *The Story of a Soul* and found in its pages new insights of mystical spirituality solidly based on the gospels that the church authorities began to appreciate that the life and teaching of this young Carmelite nun was a matter for serious official examination. Not only was the process begun, but it ended with the canonisation of Thérèse in 1925, the statutory fifty-year delay after the death of a candidate having been cut short by Pope Benedict XV, one of the three popes during whose reigns the process lasted. The Vatican could not ignore the many miracles, as well as the many other favours attributed to the intercession of Sister Thérèse of the Child Jesus – seven volumes in a series entitled *Pluie de roses (Shower of roses)* were published between 1907 and 1925, and they contained an account of only the most notable miracles and conversions.

Today, the Carmel of Lisieux is a place of pilgrimage, while crowning the hill behind it there stands the great Basilica of St Thérèse, built at the express wish of Pope Pius XI who had canonised her. It was begun in 1929 and finished in 1937. Around the world, more than 1,700 churches or chapels are dedicated to her. Among these there are eight cathedrals and five basilicas. One of these churches is situated in Cairo, and it is in itself symbolic in showing that the spiritual teachings, based on the love of God for the soul and of the soul for God, found in her writings and exemplified in her life, make Thérèse and her 'Little Way' an inspiration and a guide for anyone who believes in God, no matter what the religious milieu in which that belief grows and expresses itself: that Catholic church in Cairo was a gift offered by the Muslims of the city to 'the Little Saint of Allah' to thank her for favours received.

As a conclusion to the story of her life, Thérèse of the Little

Way to sanctity would, I trust, agree that nothing could be more fitting than the last prayer she wrote, on the back of a holy picture and with a trembling hand, just a few weeks before she died. It is a short ecstatic aspiration, addressed to Our Blessed Lady as a little gift on 8 September, her official birthday in the church calendar, and it is a prayer that encapsulates Thérèse's personal way to sainthood, childish in its expression, profound in its connotations. Let us look at it devoutly, first in the actual words in which it was written:

O Marie, si j'étais la Reine du Ciel et que vous soyez Thérèse, je voudrais être Thérèse afin que vous soyez la Reine du Ciel!

And in English:

O Mary, if I were the Queen of Heaven and you were Thérèse, I would wish to be Thérèse so that you would be the Queen of Heaven!